Walking Tours
of Old Philadelphia

Other books by Paul Hogarth

ARTIST AS REPORTER
ARTISTS ON HORSEBACK: THE OLD WEST IN ILLUSTRATED JOURNALISM
BRENDAN BEHAN'S ISLAND (with Brendan Behan)
BRENDAN BEHAN'S NEW YORK (with Brendan Behan)
DRAWING ARCHITECTURE
LONDON À LA MODE (with Malcolm Muggeridge)
LOOKING AT CHINA
MAJORCA OBSERVED (with Robert Graves)
A RUSSIAN JOURNEY (with Alaric Jacob)

PAUL HOGARTH'S
Walking Tours
of Old Philadelphia

Through Independence Square, Society Hill,
Southwark, and Washington Square

BARRE PUBLISHING
Barre, Massachusetts

DISTRIBUTED BY CROWN PUBLISHERS, INC.
NEW YORK

Inquiries should be addressed to Clarkson N. Potter, Inc., 419 Park Avenue South, New York, N.Y. 10016.

Library of Congress Cataloging in Publication Data

Hogarth, Paul, 1917-
Paul Hogarth's walking tours of old Philadelphia.

Bibliography: p.
Includes index.
1. Philadelphia—Description—1951-   —Tours.
I.   Walking tours of old Philadelphia.
F158.18.H63   1976   917.48′11′044   75-30967
ISBN 0–517–52384–1
ISBN 0–517–52385–X pbk.

If you're off to Philadelphia in the morning,
  You mustn't go by everything I've said.
Bob Bicknell's Southern Stages have been laid aside for ages,
  But the Limited will take you there instead.
Toby Hirte can't be seen at One Hundred and Eighteen
  North Second Street—no matter when you call;
And I fear you'll search in vain for the wash-house down the lane
  Where Pharaoh played the fiddle at the ball.

RUDYARD KIPLING

CONTENTS

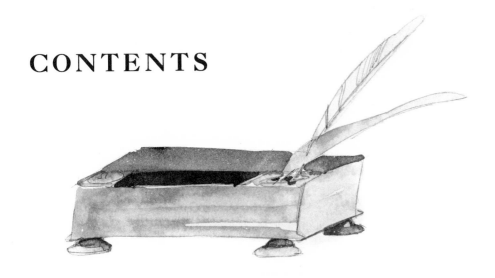

ACKNOWLEDGMENTS

For my text I have drawn heavily on previous books, notably such authoritative sources as John F. Watson's *Annals of Philadelphia* (1830), Scharf and Westcott's *History of Philadelphia* (1884), Theo B. White's *Philadelphia Architecture in the Nineteenth Century* (1953), Luther P. Eisenhart's *Historic Philadelphia* (1953), and John Francis Marion's *Bicentennial City* (1974).

I should also like to express my thanks to Charles E. Peterson, architect and historian, for friendly guidance; Whitfield J. Bell, Jr., librarian of the American Philosophical Society, for his helpful suggestions; to Richard Tyler, historian of the Philadelphia Historical Commission, for allowing me access to his invaluable files, and James E. Mooney, director of the Historical Society of Pennsylvania, for research facilities; to Sam and Lillyan Maitin for hospitality and assistance of every kind; to Ann Schubert, librarian of the Museum of the Insurance Company of North America; to Edward Riley for his help in shaping the book; and to John Stillman for his help.

My quotations from Kipling's poem ''Philadelphia'' are taken from his *Rewards and Fairies* (1910).

INTRODUCTION

by E. Digby Baltzell

For two dozen years, between the signing of the Declaration of Independence and the departure of John and Abigail Adams for the partially constructed White House in Washington, the greatest generation of American statesmen and leaders walked the streets of Philadelphia: George Washington, Thomas Jefferson, and James Madison (Dolley was a Philadelphian) of Virginia; Charles Pinckney of Charleston, South Carolina; Alexander Hamilton, John Jay, and Gouverneur Morris of New York; the Adamses, Rufus King, and John Hancock of Massachusetts; and Benjamin Franklin, Robert Morris, James Wilson, John Dickinson, and the newly arrived radical, Tom Paine, all of Philadelphia. They were individuals in the same mold as the heroes of Periclean Athens, Cicero's Rome, or Elizabethan London. Jefferson, while abroad on a diplomatic mission, looked back on the men writing our Constitution in Philadelphia and called them a "group of Demigods."

Walking around the old city, visiting the landmarks described and delightfully illustrated by Paul Hogarth in this book, one should try to visualize the lives of these founding fathers: planning and finally declaring a radical revolution at Carpenters' Hall in the spring of 1776; writing a conservative constitution in stately Independence Hall during the hot, humid summer of '87; wheeling and dealing over glasses of Madeira at the City Tavern; discussing the latest scientific subjects at the American Philosophical Society's headquarters; and perhaps dining and dancing at the invitation of the beautiful and intelligent Anne Willing Bingham, queen of the "Republican Court," as fashionable Philadelphia was called in its capital days. Her husband, the richest man in America, was soon to finance, with his son-in-law of the British house of Baring, the most famous real estate deal in our history — the Louisiana Purchase. Finally, of course, one must visualize all these ladies, gentlemen, and their families worshipping on Sunday at St. Peter's or Old Pine Church, or at Christ Church, where even Benjamin Franklin, the skeptical deist, kept a family pew.

Philadelphians were ideal hosts for the men and women of this heroic age. Ever since William Penn and his Friendly followers landed on the shores of the Delaware, the Quaker City has, with its tolerant hospitality, attracted talented men of all nations, races, and creeds— much like New York in our own day. Whereas most of the Virginia gentlemen were descendants of Anglican Cavaliers who fled from the victorious armies of Cromwell, and nearly all the Massachusetts men were descended from English Puritans, Philadelphians were part of a melting pot from the beginning. The first census in 1790 showed that though the white population of Virginia and Massachusetts was between 80 and 90 percent English, Pennsylvania was only 40 percent English, over 30 percent German, and almost 25 percent Irish or Scottish.

As one visits the many houses of worship on these walks — Greek Orthodox and Roman Catholic, Jewish, and Protestant of many denominations — one is reminded of Penn's ideals, of freedom and toleration, which anticipated the ideals of all America, as symbolized by the Statue of Liberty in New York harbor. Now, however, the same nation that once had such great expectations seems haunted by the fear that it has lost its idealism. One must hope that the Americans who walk the streets of Philadelphia today will return to their homes with a justified pride in the past, and a renewed faith in their country's ideals.

PREFACE

Around 1890, the celebrated British poet, Rudyard Kipling, visited Philadelphia. He liked the city but mourned the loss of the "American Athens." And in his poem "Philadelphia," he wrote that the old city had

. . . gone, gone, gone with the lost Atlantis,
(Never say I didn't give you warning.)
In Seventeen Ninety-three 'twas there for all to see,
But it's not in Philadelphia this morning.

Kipling was only partly right. Penn's "greene Countrie Towne," focus of all that was cosmopolitan and progressive in colonial America, had, like every other big city, succumbed to the remorseless pressures of urbanization. But unlike most other big American cities, Philadelphia had expanded sideways, leaving the old city to become a downtown business district, and worse, a fearsome slum. It was still there "for all to see"—but not to enjoy.

My stay in 1968–1969 did not dispel the shock that Philadelphia, as a city, had long since sacrificed its heritage. Since 1951 the National Park Service had carried out extensive rehabilitation of historic buildings, but in 1969 it still had a long way to go. The chaos of demolition alternated with the desolation of huge empty lots. It was difficult to imagine how Independence National Historic Park would look when completed because that time seemed so far in the future.

A second look some four years later managed to put old Philadelphia into proper perspective. At last, walking through the completed Independence Park and seeing Independence Hall, Congress Hall, Old City Hall, Carpenters' Hall, the First Bank of the United States, the Second Bank of the United States, restored Colonial houses, the Philadelphia Exchange, Christ Church, Society Hill, and much more, the scale of the task began to impress itself on my jaundiced eye. I stayed at the Benjamin Franklin Hotel and, like any other tourist, I walked about for an entire weekend. I returned to New York convinced of one thing only: Colonial Philadelphia was still there "for all to see" on *any* morning. And I had to draw it!

In the belief that artists, from the age of the Grand Tour up to the present day, have always helped to open tourists' eyes, my book is offered in the form of a guide to the places I saw and enjoyed.

Inevitably, there are omissions. It would have been an encyclopedic task to have drawn everything, so I have restricted myself to Penn's original city, resisting the temptation to include Colonial Germantown and the Colonial mansions of Fairmount Park. On six walks I have selected the more important places to see and visit, beginning with the public buildings of Independence Park and ending with the picturesque back streets west of Pennsylvania Hospital.

I have not attempted to imitate the numerous guidebooks that list theatres, museums, restaurants, hotels, and events of interest to visitors. Rather, my aim has been to inspire exploration and personal discoveries. Each walk will provide you with the general historic background of a given section, using outstanding examples of historic architecture to illuminate still further the city's unique past. For this reason I have included appendixes designed to help you focus on such details as footscrapers, hitching posts, and firemarks. For those with an appetite for such things, I have also included the names of architects, the dates of construction, and a glossary of architectural terms.

The eastern cities of the United States, and indeed many older cities in Europe, have cause to envy Philadelphia for the breadth of vision and the scale of preservation of its heritage. Thousands of old houses and many public buildings will be accessible to the public during the bicentennial celebration of 1976. I hope you will find, as I have, that walking the historic streets of colonial Philadelphia can give you a greater awareness of the role this city played in the birth of the nation. To quote Kipling again—and he was right this time:

They are there, there, there with Earth immortal.
(Citizens, I give you friendly warning.)
The things that truly last (when men and times have
*   passed,*
They are all in Pennsylvania this morning!

AUTHOR'S NOTE

Philadelphia is divided into five sections: North, South, West Philadelphia, the Northeast, and Center City. Here, we are concerned only with Center City and its southern tip, Southwark and Queen Village.

Finding your way around is made fairly simple by the checkerboard plan devised in 1682 by William Penn's surveyor, Captain Thomas Holme. Center City lies between two rivers, the Delaware on the east and the Schuylkill on the west. After Front, the first street on the Delaware, the streets running north-south are numbered Second, Third, Fourth, and so on. The only exception is Broad Street, which runs where Fourteenth Street should be. House numbers run west from Front Street, every block beginning a new hundred, with even numbers on the south side of the street.

Each of the six sections in this book begins with a map showing all the buildings I have drawn, with numbers keyed to the text. Museums or places of interest not illustrated are indicated in the text and on the maps by a star (★). The arrows indicate the direction in which I have walked (which would, of course, be reversed should you begin your walk at the opposite end). As is customary, the top of the page is north.

Walk 1

Independence
National Historic Park

DISTANCE: 1 mile. TIME: 5 to 6 hours; at least one whole day. It can also be done in 2 to 3 hours, depending on how many buildings are visited.

Of all the walks I took in historic Philadelphia, this is the one that best helped me to imagine what the city looked like between 1770 and 1834. It was, as you will see, a city pleasantly punctuated by steeples, domes, and lantern towers. Here and there the red-brick ruddiness of well-built houses is broken up by the white marble and gray stone of classical edifices with pediments and colonnades. That so much of this still exists for our enjoyment is a miracle of preservation.

Independence Park is situated largely within the four blocks bounded by Second and Sixth streets, and Chestnut and Locust. It is, of course, the most historic area in the United States, and through the park can be seen Carpenters' Hall—the scene of the First Continental Congress—flanked by New Hall. The walker experiences an extraordinary sensation of being back in post-Revolutionary times.

Leaving Carpenters' Hall, crossing Fourth Street, and continuing west along cobblestoned Library Street, you sense the special atmosphere of bygone days. You pass the fine iron railing and Doric colonnade of the Second Bank of the United States (now the Philadelphia Portrait Gallery). You stand before Library Hall, built originally for the Library Company of Philadelphia in 1789–1790, torn down in 1884, but now faithfully rebuilt on its original site.

It was in these buildings on Independence Square itself that history was made. Here Independence was declared; the Articles of Confederation were discussed, drafted, and adopted; and the Constitution of the United States was written. Within the walls of Independence Hall, Congress Hall, and Old City Hall, the foundations of federal government were established: the Supreme Court, the Second Continental Congress, the Senate, and the House of Representatives.

Also on the square is the American Philosophical Society, the oldest and most distinguished of learned societies in the New World, which has carried on its activities there since 1789. Not far away, on Orianna Street, Benjamin Franklin lived in what is now Franklin Court. Bishop William White, rector of Christ Church and St. Peter's Church, and the first Episcopal bishop of Pennsylvania, lived in the same area, on Walnut Street near Third; and John Todd and his wife Dolley, later the wife of President James Madison, lived at Fourth and Walnut streets.

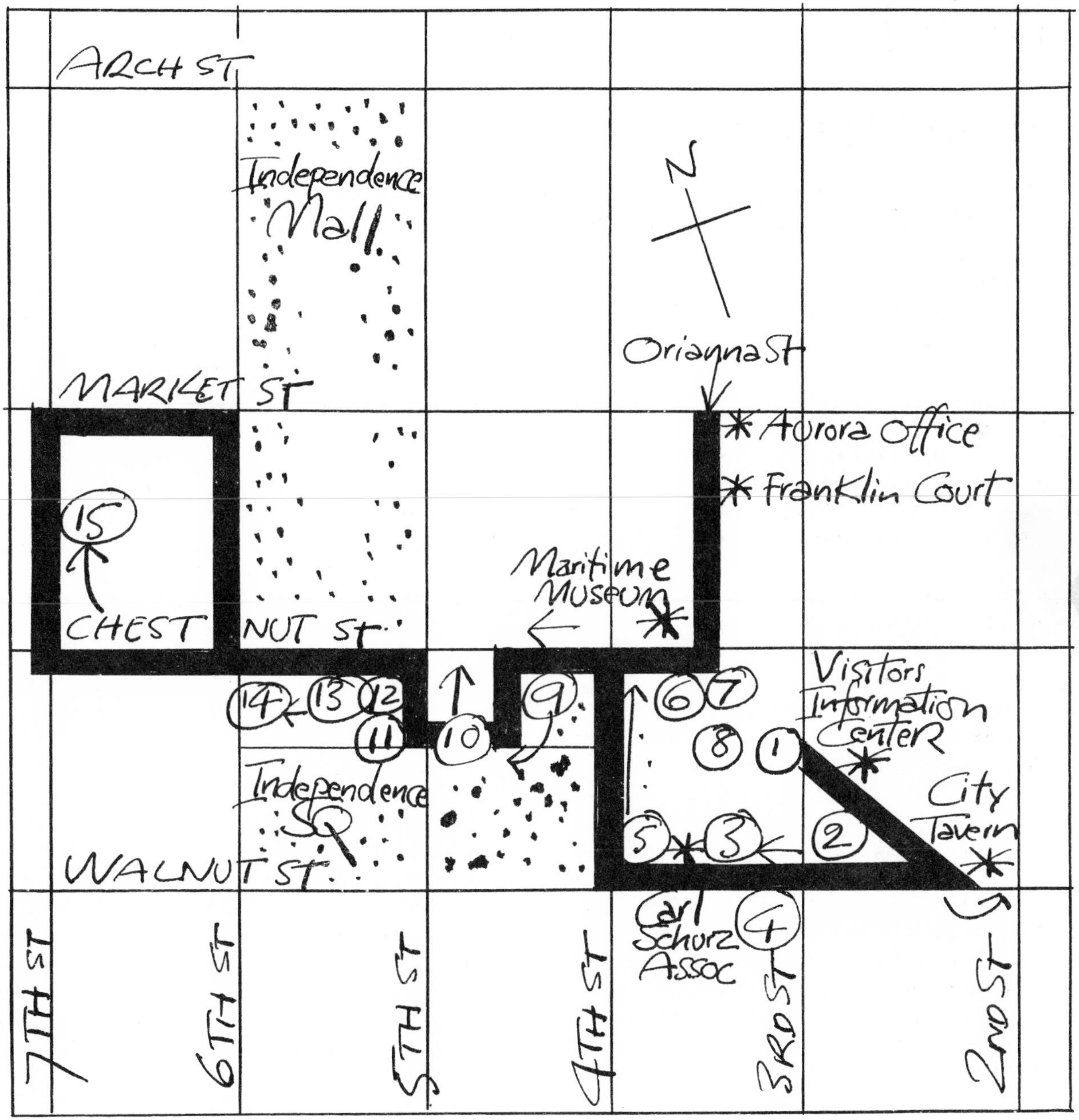

ARCH ST

Independence
Mall

N

Oriagna St

MARKET ST

* Aurora Office

* Franklin Court

15

Maritime
Museum

CHEST   NUT ST

*

14 13 12   10   9   6 7

11

Visitors
Information
Center

8   1

*

Independence

5 *   3   2

City
Tavern

*

WALNUT ST

Carl
Schurz
Assoc

4

7TH ST

6TH ST

5TH ST

4TH ST

3RD ST

2ND ST

First Bank of the United States
and the Philadelphia Exchange

First Bank of the United States: 116 South Third Street. Open daily 9:00–5:00. Free. Time: 20 minutes.

Philadelphia Exchange: Third and Walnut streets. Not open to the public. Time: allow 15 minutes for external view and visit to nearby City Tavern.

To savor this experience to the full, begin as I did at the **First Bank of the United States (1)**.

Directly opposite the Visitors Information Center (★) on South Third Street between Chestnut and Walnut, this stately edifice, the oldest bank building in the United States, was erected in 1795 – 1797 and is now a museum devoted to the history of the Treasury Department.

Remarkably enough, it was designed by an amateur, Samuel Blodget, Jr. (1749–1814), a merchant and promoter, and a cofounder of the Insurance Company of North America. Very much a man of his time, Blodget fought the British redcoats as a captain in the New Hampshire militia, serving on Washington's staff during the Siege of Boston in 1775. After the war he made a fortune in the China trade and became engaged in the development of Philadelphia about the time the city was designated the temporary capital of the country. He was also active in the planning and founding of Washington, D.C., as the federal capital. Next to founding companies and developing cities, Blodget's favorite preoccupation was designing buildings, and, being a man of taste, his designs have a well-rounded sense of style and beauty.

In 1811, the bank's charter expired and another remarkable merchant prince, Stephen Girard (1750–1831), a French immigrant who rapidly established himself in the city as a shipowner, bought the building for his Girard Bank (1812 – 1831). After Girard's death, the premises were occupied by the Girard National Bank from 1832 to 1926, and, in more recent times, by the American Legion and the Directors of the Board of City Trusts.

No more telling symbol could have been conceived for the young Republic and the confidence it sought to inspire than the Greco-Roman solidity of this superb example of the Federal style. The central projecting portico stands six steps above street level. Inside, the great rotunda, with its vast dome dominating the banking floor, has recently been restored to its original grandeur. Another notable feature is the vigorously carved American eagle on the tympanum of the pediment. Note also the ironwork—the majestic gates at each side, leading to the park and to Carpenters' Hall; the finely wrought iron footscrapers (see pages 142 – 43), and the huge ornate lantern above the portal, or front entrance.

Before you head west toward Carpenters' Hall, recross Third Street to the Visitors Information Center. Turn left into cobbled Dock Street. Facing you is the **Philadelphia Exchange (2)**, erected 1832–1834, and for over half a century the commercial hub of the city. This building of soft-toned gray stone is a superb example of the Greek Revival style which is plentiful throughout the city. Continue east a little farther and then turn around and enjoy a sweeping view of both the Exchange and the First Bank, now further enhanced by the picturesque winding street of rounded cobblestones.

The Exchange is the kind of classical building I enjoy drawing because it is rather unconventional. It was designed by William Strickland (1787–1854), a leading architect of the time, and stylishly combines a flat rectangular building with a semicircular rotunda of tall fluted columns set off by an antefix, or ornamental band, of stylized cast-iron palm leaves above the roof. It looks rather like a wedding cake and is crowned with a tall, slim, pilastered lantern tower. From this tower, ships could be seen miles away up and down the river. The cobblestone street in front is the site of Dock Creek, which originally flowed into the Delaware. Note the lions, symbols of vigilance and strength, guarding the outer stairs to the Exchange Room. They were imported from Italy and first placed there in 1838, the gift of John Moss, a Philadelphia merchant.

Until the Civil War, the Exchange was widely admired as one of the finest buildings in Philadelphia. Its decline began when it became the Corn Exchange (1866–1875), and then the Stock Exchange (1875–1900). The Greek Revival style finally lost favor in the Gilded Age. After the Stock Exchange moved to more splendid quarters, it became the Produce Exchange (1922–1950). The lions were removed and the outside stairs pulled down. Market sheds were put up and a gas station was built on its north side. Some Philadelphians remember with nostalgia that they were taken there as children to buy Christmas trees and wreaths. The building continued to decline, but in 1952 it was miraculously rescued and taken over by the National Park Service to form part of Independence Park.

Behind you is **City Tavern** (★), a reconstruction on the original site of a celebrated Philadelphia meeting place. Built in 1773, it was a favorite base for colonial merchants, and later, revolutionaries, offering board and lodging and well-appointed rooms for banquets and balls. Much of the wheeling and dealing between various political factions that preceded the Declaration of Independence was either planned or celebrated here.

Old Original Bookbinders, at 125 Walnut Street and conveniently close to City Tavern, is one of Philadelphia's justifiably famous and highly recommended seafood restaurants.

The watch boxes outside the First Bank and the Exchange (Dock Street) are reconstructions based on a type known to exist in the 1790s, and used by the watchmen who guarded the buildings. Watchmen also kept a sharp lookout for fires, a vital precaution in view of the primitive methods of dealing with fires at that time.

Bishop White House

309 Walnut Street. Open daily 9:00–5:00. Inquire at Visitors Information Center, South Third Street, for times and tickets for free guided tours that take place at frequent intervals. Time: 30 minutes.

Proceed west on Walnut toward Fourth to the **Bishop White House (3)**, erected 1786–1787 by the Right Reverend William White (1748–1836), first bishop of the Episcopal Church in the United States. He was also chaplain of the Continental Congress and later of the United States Senate, and was therefore a public figure of some importance. The Park Service has done an impressive job of restoring the house to its condition during the fifty years Bishop White and his family (five children and eleven grandchildren) lived in its airy and elegant rooms.

Everything about this charming house reflects the life-style of a sophisticated, cultured clergyman who entertained everyone of importance in the city. Much original material was actually found inside the house itself; the original front door was brought to light from the cellars, and bits of silver and tableware were unearthed in archaeological excavations of the drainage system. The furniture and fixtures are of the period. Many are original family heirlooms: for example, the two fine portraits of the bishop's grandparents by Sir Godfrey Kneller (c. 1646–1723), and also a portrait of the bishop himself by the Philadelphia painter Charles Willson Peale (1741–1827). Thanks to a contemporary painting by the Philadelphia artist-engraver John Sartain, even the bishop's study has been restored to its original state as well as his personal library.

Directly opposite the Bishop White House is the elegant classical facade of what was the first building of the **Philadelphia Savings Fund Society Bank (4)**, 306 Walnut Street. Not open to the public. Built in 1840, it was designed by one of Philadelphia's best known architects, Thomas Ustick Walter (1804–1887) of Capitol dome fame. The oldest savings bank in America, the Savings Fund Society Bank was founded in 1816 by Colonel Condy Raguet, who modeled it on the savings banks popular at the time in England. The building is currently occupied by a casualty insurance company, but much of the fine ornamental plasterwork has been left in place.

Back on the north side of Walnut, the houses along the rest of the block to the west are also restorations or reconstructions. Nos. 311 and 313 are the offices of the Independence National Park Service where the Park Service's historians carry on their good work. No. 315 is occupied by the Pennsylvania Horticultural Society (1812), the oldest horticultural society in the United States, whose activities have included the planting of several colonial and Victorian gardens in the area. At the side of the building is an eighteenth-century garden complete with gazebo and orchard. Nos. 339 and 341, reconstructions of the Morris and Griffith houses (1775), are occupied by the **National Carl Schurz Association (★)**. (Open 9:00–5:00 Monday through Friday. Free.) Reformer Carl Schurz, most eminent of nineteenth-century German Americans, fought in the Civil War and served as Secretary of the Interior under President Hayes. The association has an interesting collection of paintings and memorabilia illustrating the German contribution to American life and culture.

Philadelphia Savings Fund Society Bank. 306 Walnut Street.

Todd-Moylan House

Northeast corner, Fourth and Walnut streets. Open in summer Tuesday through Saturday 10:00–7:00; Sunday 1:00–4:00. In winter: Tuesday through Friday 11:00–7:00. Free guided tours every 15 minutes. Time: 15 minutes.

The **Todd-Moylan House (5)** was built in 1775 by John Dilworth. John Todd, a promising young lawyer, bought the house in 1791 and lived there with his wife, Dolley Payne Todd, until his death from yellow fever in 1793. His pretty young widow later met and married James Madison, then a member of the House of Representatives. When the British raided Washington in 1814, it was Dolley Madison who managed to save the White House silver. Stephen Moylan, the Revolutionary War general, also lived in the Todd-Moylan house 1796–1807.

Although smaller and much more modest than the Bishop White House, the Todd-Moylan house is no less interesting as an example of a middle-class home of the period. Once again the Park Service is to be congratulated. The house has been restored (for some years it was a luncheonette and corner store) and furnished as it was during the years the Todds lived there. A complete inventory was discovered and many original pieces tracked down in various museums and private collections; those not found were replaced with similar items.

The house is the end-of-row type characteristic of Pennsylvania, Delaware, and New Jersey. The front door is placed on one side. My picture shows it thus and includes the garden behind with its pump. Note the laundry deck above the kitchen on the left.

New Hall, Pemberton House, and Carpenters' Hall

Between Third and Fourth streets on Chestnut. New Hall: open in summer 9:00–4:45. In winter: Wednesday through Sunday 9:00–4:45, and on alternate Mondays and Tuesdays in rotation with Pemberton House. Free. Time: 10–15 minutes.

Walk north on Fourth to Chestnut, turn right into Chestnut and enter Carpenters' Hall Court. To the right is **New Hall (6)**, originally built by the Carpenters' Company in 1790 for rental income, and occupied by the War Department of the young Republic, 1791–1792. Now reconstructed, it houses the Marine Corps Memorial Museum. The sequence of exhibits dates from the Leathernecks of 1775 to the Barbary Wars of 1801–1815.

Across from New Hall, just before the gates of Carpenters' Court, is **Pemberton House (7)**. The tall three-story house in my picture is a reconstruction of the home of Quaker merchant James Joseph Pemberton, originally built on the site in 1775. It is a museum that tells the story of the early days of the army and navy (1775–1805), using diagrams, old flags, tapes, maps, and weapons.

Carpenters' Hall (8), 320 Chestnut Street. The square building with the weather vane is very much the real thing. Here the First Continental Congress met in September 1774 while the building was still being finished. Many historic decisions were taken, the most important being that of establishing revolutionary leadership and founding a system of democratic government. As the afternoon sun goes

down and lengthening shadows envelop the straight-backed colonial chairs, it is possible to imagine the delegates sitting there attentively absorbed in the debates. Robert Smith (1722–1777), a well-known architect and carpenter, is thought to have designed the building. Carpenters' Hall is still owned by the Carpenters' Company, and they use it four times a year for their regular meetings.

Cross Chestnut Street to the **Philadelphia Maritime Museum** (★), 321 Chestnut Street, directly opposite Pemberton House. Open Monday through Saturday 10:00–5:00; Sunday 12:00–5:00. Time: allow 45 minutes.

Here is a fascinating collection that reveals the prime reasons for much of the early development that made Philadelphia the second largest city of the British Empire after London. There are models of ships from the eighteenth century down to the present day; and also naval weapons, charts, and whaling gear.

As you exit the museum, turn left into Orianna Street. In this little alley is **Franklin Court** (★), where Benjamin Franklin lived and where he died in 1790, aged 84. There isn't much to see other than the archaeological dig that uncovered many artifacts and revealed the great man's passion for Madeira. The Park Service decided not to attempt a reconstruction as too little information about the house could be found, but the site itself has been developed, with gardens and the plane and mulberry trees that Franklin himself favored. **No. 322 Market Street** (★), designed by Franklin, was originally the business office of *Aurora*, the newspaper published by his grandson, Benjamin Franklin Bache. Nos. 316 and 318 were also designed by Franklin. In these buildings exhibits and films about Franklin are shown. Inquire at the Visitors Information Center for further details.

12

Second Bank of the United States

420 Chestnut Street. Open daily 10:00–5:00. Free. Time: 30–45 minutes.

Cross back to the south side of Chestnut and continue west across Fourth. On your left between Fourth and Fifth is the Doric-columned **Second Bank of the United States (9)**. Designed by William Strickland in 1818 and built in 1819–1824, it is without doubt one of the finest examples of Greek Revival architecture in the United States. Strickland's patron at the time was the urbane Nicholas Biddle (1786–1844), president of the bank. It was at Biddle's suggestion that a Grecian style was adopted for the new building. The model was the Parthenon, whose proportions and style Strickland sought to reconcile with modern needs. That he succeeded admirably can be seen in the beautifully lit great banking hall with its intricate barrel-vaulted ceiling.

The Second Bank occupied the building from its completion in 1824 until 1836, when President Andrew ("Old Hickory") Jackson vetoed the bill to renew its charter. Although the bank continued under a state charter until 1841, it was dead—a great loss to Philadelphia. Charles Dickens, visiting the city in 1841, expressed the same opinion. On the night of his arrival, Dickens looked out on "a handsome building of white marble, which had a mournful ghost-like aspect." He attributed this impression to the somber influence of the night, and fancied that in the morning its steps would be thronged with people passing in and out. When he saw no such scene, he asked about the building and was told it was the "tomb of many fortunes," the Great Catacomb of investments, the memorable Second Bank of the United States. The closing of the bank, with all its ominous consequences, had cast a gloom on the city.

Be that as it may, the Second Bank today presents an animated spectacle as visitors throng the steps. This handsome building now houses the Faces of Independence, a remarkable collection of portraits of colonial and federal leaders, largely by Charles Willson Peale, whose dream of a National Portrait Gallery for his paintings has at long last been realized. Here can be seen portraits of the signers of the Declaration of Independence and of the Constitution, and a host of political and military leaders, scientists, artists, merchants, and diplomats, all of whom helped shape America.

As fascinating as this pictorial history undoubtedly is, only the most determined visitor will stay the entire course, not to say absorb all that is offered in the way of biographical information. For most of us the multitude of faces can lull the senses to the point of fatigue after fifteen minutes. I found it wiser to take only a section or two; the signers of the Declaration of Independence and the Constitution, for example, and Washington. But I found myself going back a second time to study the officers of the Revolution, foreign dignitaries, American statesmen, and figures in the War of 1812. Names thus acquired have greater meaning because one has gazed upon the faces—an advantage when I finally arrived at Independence Hall to take the guided tour.

As you leave the Second Bank, walk south on Chestnut through the passage to the left of the bank. This brings you to cobbled Library Street and a vista of green stretching south to Walnut Street. Note the statue of Robert Morris, banker and financier of the Revolution. Continue west along Library Street. On the right is **Library Hall (10)**.

The original building was torn down in 1884 and reconstructed in 1959. The new building is an exact replica of the first, even to the statue of Franklin over the front entrance. The original sculpture, by François Lazzarini, very chipped and weather-beaten, is preserved at the Library Company, 1314 Locust Street.

Library Hall now houses the reading rooms of the American Philosophical Society, founded by Franklin and his friends in 1743, as well as a library justly world-famous as one of the principal institutions in the United States for the study of the history of the sciences. Here can be found rare volumes, such as first editions of Newton's *Principia*, Franklin's *Experiments and Observations*, and Darwin's *Origin of Species*. Outstanding manuscript collections of special importance are those devoted to the history, customs, and languages of the American Indian, including the original journals of the Lewis and Clark expedition of 1804–1806. There is also a unique collection of watercolors and pencil sketches by Titian Ramsay Peale who, with Samuel Seymour, accompanied Major Long's expedition to explore the Western plains, the "Great American Desert," as it was called in those days.

Libraries are the means by which the dynamic of progress is maintained. For example, three versions of the Declaration of Independence, that historic document that moved the world on to a new and higher stage of human endeavor, are still preserved intact in Library Hall. The first is a broadside on vellum that once belonged to David Rittenhouse. The second is a contemporary broadside on paper, probably the one read publicly by Colonel John Nixon on July 8, 1776. The third and most important of all is the manuscript copy in Jefferson's own handwriting with notes by Richard Henry Lee and Arthur Lee.

The designer of the original Library Hall, William Thornton, was a young physician, educated in Edinburgh, London, and Paris, who had recently arrived in Philadelphia. Doctors of medicine, like merchant princes and carpenters, might also be architects in those days. The young doctor had no architectural training and the design for the library was the first he made. In those days a well-developed sense of style (cultivated by travel), a trained talent for drawing (involving a study of architecture), and a grasp of mathematics were enough for an intelligent man to apply himself to the task. The motivating factor was an overwhelming desire to contribute to an important enterprise. Later, young Thornton won the competition to design the United States Capitol in Washington and eventually he left Philadelphia to become the commissioner of the new federal city.

A building of stately elegance, Library Hall stands quite apart from most other public buildings of the period. This is partly because of its setting and its relationship to the surrounding buildings. My picture (pages 16–17) shows the front of the library on South Fifth Street set against a skyline of pediments, trees, and lantern towers. The cobbled street takes the eye back to distant Carpenters' Hall standing within a walled garden of shrubs and trees. But this is also partly because of its inherent grace of design. A pedimented facade of pilasters rises two stories above the entrance, fringed at the roof line with a balustrade of urns. The inspired final touch, the statue of Franklin, is secure in its niche of immortality.

The library is open to serious scholars for research and reference work, but anyone may look at the changing exhibits usually displayed in the lobby.

Almost opposite the Fifth Street entrance to Library Hall and situated on Independence Square is **Philosophical Hall (11)**, the headquarters of the American Philosophical Society.

Library Hall

105 South Fifth Street. Open Monday through Friday 9:00–5:00.

This building was erected 1785–1789 and is worth gazing at to reflect on its illustrious past. Since 1785 it has housed the oldest learned society in America; like the Pennsylvania Hospital, the University of Pennsylvania, the Philadelphia Contributionship, and many other Philadelphia institutions, it was started by Benjamin Franklin.

The society has played the vital role of "think tank" in the United States for more than two centuries. During all this time, except when the British army occupied Philadelphia during the Revolutionary War, the society has met regularly to discuss discoveries of importance. Membership included not only doctors, lawyers, clergymen, and merchants interested in the sciences to the point of obsession, but also self-taught artisans and tradesmen like Franklin. It was, therefore, more democratic than its counterpart, the Royal Society of London. Most of the Founding Fathers were members: Washington, Thomas Jefferson, Alexander Hamilton, Thomas Paine, Benjamin Rush, James Madison, and John Marshall; as were British scientists like Joseph Priestley, whom Franklin encouraged to emigrate to America; and many distinguished foreign partisans of liberty: Lafayette, Steuben, and Kosciusko.

Philosophy as a discipline was far more inclusive in the eighteenth century than today. In those days philosophy included scientific and technological knowledge, particularly that which would enable the American colonies and states to achieve greater self-sufficiency. In this building the society discussed new and better ways of raising such crops as silk, extracting oil from sunflower seeds, canal-building, astronomy, and developing laborsaving devices— in a land where labor was always in short supply.

The role of the American Philosophical Society assumed even greater importance after Independence, when Philadelphia became the political capital of the nation, 1775–1800, and the cultural capital for many years afterward. In the absence of any federal organization, presidents, secretaries of state, military and naval commanders frequently consulted the society on such diverse subjects as the topography of the Western territories, Indian customs, coastal and land surveys. Technological progress depended a great deal on the work of the society, which truly "fulfilled the functions of a national academy of science, a national library, and even a patent office," by keeping in touch with a legion of scientists, both professional and amateur.

Inside, a graceful marble staircase ascends to the main hall, which has been sympathetically remodeled with the rest of the interior. Prints and memorabilia abound and provide the feeling of tradition. But it is the society's collection of portraits that enables the viewer to appreciate the forceful personalities of the men whose ideas so radically transformed America.

Here is a fine portrait of Washington by Gilbert Stuart; and my own personal favorite is the superb Jefferson by Thomas Sully. There is, too, the celebrated "thumb" portrait of Franklin, supposedly reading a paper sent by the British scientist Sir William Alexander; it is Charles Willson Peale's copy of the original by David Martin, now in the White House. Some of these paintings and other treasures of the society can be seen at the Historical Society of Pennsylvania, 1300 Locust Street, where the Historical Society, Philosophical Society, and Library Company will present a special bicentennial exhibition of their holdings. Check with the Visitors Information Center for hours.

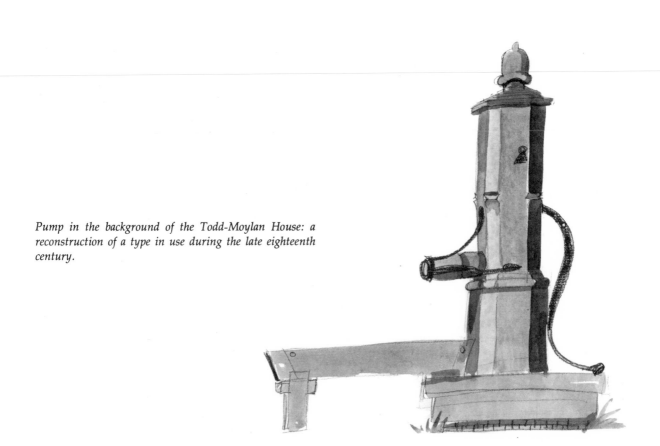

Pump in the background of the Todd-Moylan House: a reconstruction of a type in use during the late eighteenth century.

Philosophical Hall

104 South Fifth Street.
Not open to the public.

Philosophical Hall and Old City Hall (East Front).

Old City Hall

Southwest corner, Fifth and Chestnut streets. Open daily 9:00–5:00. Free. Time: 20–30 minutes.

On the southwest corner of Fifth and Chestnut, directly in front of Philosophical Hall and to the east of Independence Hall, is **Old City Hall (12)**, built 1790–1791 by the City of Philadelphia. When Philadelphia became the temporary capital, the newly completed building was offered to the federal government and housed the Supreme Court of the United States, 1791–1800. A homely, boxlike structure with a peaked roof and cupola in the middle, it was eventually used as a City Hall until the city fathers moved into the huge Victorian edifice at Broad and Market on Center Square in 1874.

Old City Hall was neglected until 1922, when it was restored to its early appearance to serve as a museum. In 1973–1974 it was again restored by the Park Service, this time to its original splendor during the early days of the Supreme Court. It is still a museum, but with a difference. On the first floor a slide presentation with sound briefly outlines some of the more important decisions of the Court. The second floor is a multimedia chronicle of the social and cultural life during the colonial and post-Revolutionary periods.

To your left as you leave Old City Hall you will notice a reconstructed colonial watchbox. This one and others in and around the Independence Hall complex are placed at the spots where boxes are known to have stood in those days.

ARTH

The Independence Hall Group

Between Fifth and Sixth streets on Chestnut. All three buildings open daily 9:00–5:00. (Independence Hall is open 8:15A.M.–8:00P.M. from July 1 through Labor Day.) Free guided tours start at the Visitors Information Center, West Wing (facing Independence Square), every 20 minutes. Time: 20–30 minutes for each building.

I began my picture on a crisp Saturday morning in the fall. The sun was rising, illuminating the clock steeple and topping the tower of Independence Hall with its golden rays. I had intended to draw only Independence Hall but the whole group, including Old City Hall and Congress Hall, stood so proudly together, I decided to draw them all. After all, they are the most important group of buildings in the early history of the United States.

All three buildings were originally erected to house the growing needs of provincial and city government. But from 1790 to 1800 the needs of the infant nation were even greater. City Hall (far left) became the Supreme Court building. Independence Hall (center), built 1732 – 1756 as the State House of Pennsylvania, became the turbulent scene of the Continental Congress and the Congress of Confederation. Here, after stormy debate, Independence was declared and the Articles of Confederation and Union agreed upon; and here, in 1787, the Constitution of the United States was written.

Congress Hall (far right), at the northwest corner of the square, was built (1787 – 1789) as the Philadelphia County Court House, and it served as the meeting place of the United

24

States Congress, the House of Representatives sitting on the first floor and the Senate on the second. I will return to this small and exquisite building again (see page 32).

Walk around Independence Hall before going inside. Stroll along the front, pausing briefly at the statue of Washington erected in 1869. Although the sculptor, I. A. Bailey, gives us a somewhat effeminate rendition of the great man, it is a pleasing enough feature. The statue is flanked by a pair of pine-cased pumps of a design common in the mid-eighteenth century (see page 31). Cross Chestnut to look at the hall from the vantage point of Independence Hall, to appreciate its qualities of symmetry and grace.

Independence Hall (13) itself was built after a design approved and supervised by Andrew Hamilton (1676–1741), an eminent lawyer and Speaker of the Assembly. He is thought to have been the architect, although some historians bestow the honor on Edmund Woolley, master carpenter. Whoever the architect was, he fulfilled his task with distinction. The classical qualities of order and balance are well expressed with solidity and elegance; a tribute also to the carpenters and stone masons who built the structure.

Perhaps the pièce de résistance of Independence Hall is the great clock with its ornate dial-plate built by Isaiah Lukens. This was originally part of the west wall, or gable, in 1752 but was removed in 1828. In 1972 it was replaced with a replica by the Park Service.

Recross Chestnut Street. Walk through the arcade to the south entrance of the West Wing, looking on to Independence Square. Here is an information center with rest rooms and telephones. The square itself (the former State House Yard), with its fine old trees, makes a

pleasantly shaded setting for Stephen Murray's vigorous statue of John Barry (1745–1803), an Irish-born Philadelphian, who was the first great naval commander to sail under the Stars and Stripes, and the "Father of the United States Navy."

To the left as you enter the hall by the front entrance is the **Pennsylvania Assembly Room**, where the delegates from the Thirteen Colonies gathered on July 4, 1776, to discuss and adopt the Declaration of Independence. Here you will see the chair used by Washington during the Constitutional Convention, with the rising sun carved on its back, and the silver inkstand (see p. vii) made by Philip Syng in 1752 and used for the signing of both the Declaration of Independence and the Constitution.

This plain and spacious chamber has been restored to its original appearance: chairs, tables covered with green baize cloth, pewter inkstands, and brass candlesticks are all of the period. My drawing (see page 30) depicts the table of the three delegates from Pennsylvania.

On the other side, to the right of the hall, is the chamber of the Pennsylvania Supreme Court with its buff-colored walls and impressive coat-of-arms above the Judge's Bench. The laws of England were the order of the day here until the Revolution, and for the rest of the eighteenth century. The prisoner's dock, jury box, and lawyer's table seem strangely empty, as though the court had just adjourned for the day.

The historic **Liberty Bell** confronts us in the stairwell of the bell tower. The original bell was ordered in London from the Whitechapel Bell Foundry in 1752 to commemorate those fifty years of religious and civil freedom under William Penn's liberal charter. The superintendents of the State House (as Independence Hall

28

was then called) selected a passage from Leviticus XXV, 10: "Proclaim liberty throughout all the land, unto all the inhabitants thereof." The bell was a source of worry and expense before it became an inspiration. It was tested shortly after its arrival in August 1752, and it cracked. A new bell was then *twice* cast by the Philadelphians John Pass and John Stow and finally hung in June 1753. It was rung to call the Assembly together, for the convening of the Continental Congress, and the opening of court. It was not rung on July 4, 1776, as legend has it, but on July 8, to summon the citizens of Philadelphia to State House Yard to hear the Declaration of Independence proclaimed by Colonel John Nixon.

Although unlucky with the original Liberty Bell, the Whitechapel Bell Foundry is still very much in business and has recently made 2,400 replicas of the Liberty Bell—one for each month of freedom — for the bicentenary celebrations. Casts were made as in 1752 with but one change: electronic equipment was used to get the right notes and tones.

At this point you have the option of leaving the tour; in fact, many do, as the venerated Liberty Bell provides something of a climax. I would urge you to continue, however, as there is more to enjoy.

Ascend the elegant staircase. To your left is the **Governor's Council Chamber**. This is where the sons and grandsons of William

Penn, or their representatives, presided over the Provincial Council. Here in his handsome room, the Proprietary Governor officially received new members of the Pennsylvania Assembly, foreign dignitaries, and Indian delegations. Most of this formality came to an end with Independence. Similar authority was vested in a Supreme Executive Council. Franklin, whose career of dedicated public service was crowned by election as president of the State of Pennsylvania, was also chosen as council president, an office that corresponds with the present governorship.

The spacious **Long Gallery** claims our attention next. Here balls and banquets honored events of importance, one of the greatest being the dinner for five hundred guests on September 16, 1774, to honor members of the First Continental Congress. During the British occupation of 1777 – 1778, this room and others were used as a military hospital; and it was here that Peale installed his museum after leaving Philosophical Hall.

Independence Hall. Reconstruction of a pump that stood here during the Colonial period.

Congress Hall

Southeast corner, Sixth and Chestnut streets. Open daily 9:00–5:00. Free guided tours. Inquire at Visitors Information Center, West Wing, Independence Hall. Time: at least 30 minutes.

Thanks to a carefully researched restoration, **Congress Hall (14)** looks much as it did when the first Congress of the United States met there (1790–1800) before the government moved to the District of Columbia. You may admire the simple lines of this compact, functional building and wonder who its designer was. But this remains a mystery. None of the original plans or drawings have been found.

On the first floor is the **House of Representatives Chamber**, handsomely furnished with semicircular mahogany tables and studded elbow chairs. Dark green valances and venetian blinds adorn the well-proportioned windows. To the right and left of the door, with its handsome fanlight, steeply inclined staircases lead to the second-floor landing with its superb view of Chestnut Street and Independence Mall. The **Senate Chamber** is even more elegantly appointed. The Speaker's rostrum with its richly crimson canopy is matched by the red-leather chairs and mahogany desks. There is also the added embellishment of a splendid fresco painting of the American eagle rising with confidence.

As I gazed out on to the tiny wrought-iron balcony outside the center front window on the second floor, I couldn't help thinking of the many distinguished notables who had gripped its top rail. Many events of importance took place here: Washington was inaugurated for his second term as president, and John Adams took his oath as second president in 1797. It was in Congress Hall that the First Bank of the United States and the Federal Mint were established by the brilliant secretary of the treasury, the short-lived Alexander Hamilton (1755 – 1804), who, in the words of Daniel Webster, "smote the rock of national resources and abundant streams of revenue gushed forth." Here also, John Jay's controversial treaty with England was debated and finally ratified. And it was here that the federal government dealt with the armed revolt against Washington's administration in 1794, which was caused by the tax Hamilton had clapped on whisky made by the farmers of western Pennsylvania to sell in the East.

Congress Hall had a much less colorful career after the federal capital was moved from Philadelphia to Washington in 1800. It reverted to the purpose for which it was originally built, and throughout the nineteenth century, federal, state, and local courts held sessions here. But by 1895 all had outgrown the tiny colonial building. Congress Hall was abandoned and fell into disrepair until its final resurrection in 1900 as a showplace of American history.

Atwater-Kent Museum

15 South Seventh Street. Open daily 8:30 – 4:00. Closed Mondays, except holidays. Free. Time: allow 45 minutes to 1 hour.

From Congress Hall, walk one block west to Seventh Street. Cross Chestnut Street and continue half a block north. The **Atwater-Kent Museum (15)** is on your right. Devoted exclusively to the history of Philadelphia, this museum is particularly interesting for its architecture and for the collections of American folk art, artifacts, games, and utensils, which had graced the houses of Philadelphians for over two centuries. There is something for everyone here and the children will enjoy the Old Toy Shop. One permanent exhibit, which illustrates the development of the city, mainly by means of prints and dioramas, should provide background for many future walks.

Originally the home of the Franklin Institute, founded in 1824 to promote scientific and technical education, this Greek Revival building was designed by John Haviland (1792–1852) and erected 1825–1827. Haviland was an Englishman who became one of Philadelphia's leading architects. On completing his studies in London, he visited Russia where he had hoped for an appointment. After a time he decided to try his luck in the United States, and arrived here in 1816. He became a successful and influential figure, and his lectures at the Franklin Institute comprised the first courses of professional architectural training in America. Haviland also designed many well known prisons throughout Pennsylvania and New York, including the Eastern Penitentiary, once the last word in prison planning, and the old Halls of Justice (the Tombs) in New York City.

The museum, one of Haviland's earlier works, is a building of unusual character, which suggests the influence of the starkly monumental style of classical St. Petersburg, Russia. Dividing its dark, brooding graystone frontage are four square-sided pilasters, heavy and projecting like buttresses. It is a frontage of great dignity and simplicity, enlivened only by a frieze of wreaths under the pediment and Old Glory flapping gently in the breeze.

Walk 2

Elfreth's Alley and Points North

DISTANCE: 2 miles. TIME: 3 to 5 hours, depending on how many buildings are visited. If you have only a limited amount of time, it would be best to make Walk 1 and then pick up part of Walk 2 for a visit to, say, Christ Church, Elfreth's Alley, the Betsy Ross House, and the Arch Street Friends Meeting House. You will have covered the most important historical sites.

The walk to the north and east of Market Street presents something of a contrast to the Georgian atmosphere of Independence National Historic Park. Nevertheless, it is full of interesting places to visit and covers a historic old part of the city. Growing toward the west from its starting point on the Delaware, the Quaker City became an important Atlantic seaport. Much that is reminiscent of the eighteenth century still remains. Here, you will find the robust flavor of a port. Cast-iron Victorian warehouses jostle against those of earlier vintage. Many had to be razed before the more

leisurely process of urban renewal could be applied. The razing even helped at times. Christ Church, for example, a justly celebrated gem of Colonial church architecture, long hidden from view by buildings on the north side of Market can now be seen in all its original splendor. Domestic architecture — the Betsy Ross House, the houses in Elfreth's Alley — is much more modest compared to that seen in Independence Park and in Society Hill on Walks 3 and 4. North of Market, like Southwark in Walk 5, was a part of the city inhabited mostly by craftsmen and artisans practicing a range of trades from printing to stonemasonry and candlemaking.

Here also you will find evidence of religious diversity and freedom in such historic landmarks as the Old First Reformed Church, St. Augustine's Roman Catholic Church, Old St. George's Methodist Church, the Free Quaker Meeting House, and the Arch Street Friends Meeting House.

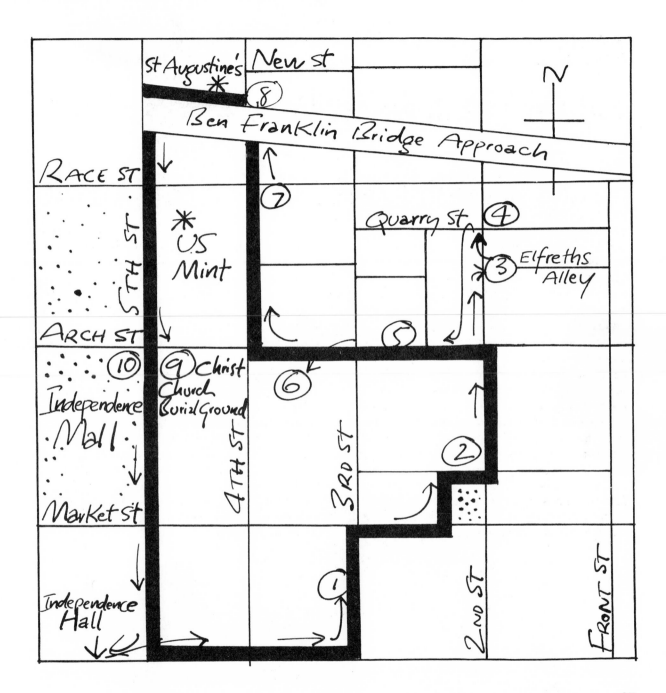

St Augustine's New St

Ben Franklin Bridge Approach

N

RACE ST

5TH ST

* US Mint

ARCH ST

⑦

Quarry St. ④

③ Elfreths Alley

⑤

⑧

⑩ ⑨ Christ Church Burial Ground

⑥

Independence Mall

4TH ST

3RD ST

②

Market St

①

2ND ST

FRONT ST

Independence Hall

Norwegian Seamen's Church

22 South Third Street. Not open to the public.

Start from Independence Hall. Walk east on Chestnut, passing the Second Bank of the United States and Carpenters' Hall Court, to Third Street. Cross Chestnut and continue north on Third. On the west side—you may even see a group of seamen talking outside—is the **Norwegian Seamen's Church (1)**, another of William Strickland's Greek Revival buildings. Once the Mechanics Bank (until 1904), it was occupied by the Citizens Bank (1919–1921), the State Bank of Pennsylvania (1921–1923), and since 1930, the Norwegian Seamen's Church.

Built in 1837, it is a fine example of Strickland's work—a design of dignity superbly expressed by four huge Corinthian pillars atop a flight of granite steps. Strickland himself was the son of a house carpenter. He was born in Philadelphia and was a pupil of the celebrated architect Benjamin Henry Latrobe, who was in charge of the restoration of the Capitol in Washington from 1815 to 1817. Considered by Niklaus Pevsner to be the most vigorous exponent of Greek Revival in the United States, Strickland loved columns and used them without stint on every possible occasion. His greatest triumphs still stand: the Second Bank of the United States, and the Philadelphia Exchange. He was also the designer of the steeple of Independence Hall for the restoration of 1828, and the Washington sarcophagus at Mount Vernon.

My picture was painted at the end of Veterans Day, shortly before the United States and Norwegian flags were lowered—a welcome splash of color against the severe gray-stone facade.

Christ Church

Second Street above Market. Open daily 9:00–5:00. Free guided tours. Time: 15 minutes; more if you saunter among the tombstones reading the inscriptions.

Leaving the Norwegian Seamen's Church on Third, cross Market and walk east to Second. Soon you will see the slender white steeple of **Christ Church (2)**, long reputed to be the highest on the North American continent, at the northwest corner of Second and Market.

For well over half a century Christ Church was the only Anglican church in the city. Bishop White, whose house you visited on Walk 1, was rector from 1779 to 1836. The present building was erected between 1727 and 1744, designed by Dr. John Kearsley, a vestryman and physician, and replaced a smaller church built in 1695. But the 200-foot-high steeple, said to have been partly designed by Franklin, was not added until 1754.

Apart from its importance as a jewel of Colonial architecture, Christ Church has a rich backlog of associations with Independence. Pewholders included such notables as Benjamin Franklin (although he rarely used it), Robert Morris, the Stow family, Philip Syng, Colonel John Nixon, and many more.

Inside the church itself is the tomb of Bishop White and the pews where George and Martha Washington and John and Abigail Adams sat. The old mahogany baptismal font, at which many notables were baptized, was brought from England in 1697. General Charles Lee is buried in the churchyard, even though he specifically requested in his will that he not be buried within a mile of any church.

The Tower Room is the starting point of the tour. Guides take you into the exquisite interior and tell of the church and its history. The room is a museum in itself, the exhibits changing each month to commemorate a special date—Franklin's birthday, for example, during the month of January. A part of Christ Church's famous Bray Library is also on display, along with many other treasures.

Above the Tower Room are the famous bells of Christ Church, cast by the Whitechapel Bell Foundry. Brought from England in 1754 by Captain Richard Budden in Nathan Levy's ship, *Myrtilla*, they were rung every time the captain weighed or cast anchor in the Delaware; and they are still rung for his descendants on request.

Elfreth's Alley

Between Arch and Race, Front and Second streets. The Elfreth's Alley Association Museum at No. 126 is open in the summer only. Telephone WA 5-0934 for hours. Time: 20 minutes.

From Christ Church continue north on busy Second Street. Just beyond Arch Street on your right, and hidden among warehouses and wholesale supply stores, is a cobbled street of ancient houses known as **Elfreth's Alley (3)**.

Dating back to 1690, it is said to be the oldest continuously occupied residential street in the United States. It is named for blacksmith Jeremiah Elfreth; and the butchers, bakers, and candlestick-makers of colonial Philadelphia lived and sometimes plied their trade here. The oldest surviving houses are thought to be Nos. 122 and 124, built between 1725 and 1727. Some of these old houses are occupied by the descendants of the original families who lived there and are not open to the public except on Elfreth's Alley Day, the first Saturday in June. At other times, you can get an idea of these old homes by visiting No. 126, the Mantua Maker's House, the small museum maintained by the Elfreth's Alley Association and containing period furniture and interesting memorabilia.

My picture was drawn from the entrance to Bladen's Court, which you should not miss; it opens off Elfreth's Alley near the Front Street exit.

From the west end of Elfreth's Alley, stroll a little farther north along Second to Quarry Street. Here, in the former headquarters of Engine Company 8, is the city's **Museum of the Fire Department (4)** where rare pieces are assembled of hand- and horse-drawn fire-fighting apparatus, firemarks from old houses, parade hats, and leather buckets. Open daily 10:00–4:00. Closed Mondays. Free. Time: allow 20–25 minutes.

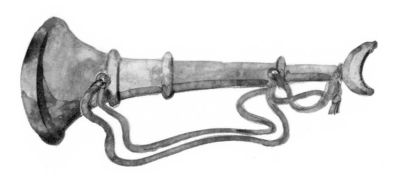

Brass trumpet, or "work horn," 1790. Philadelphia Fire Museum.

Betsy Ross House

239 Arch Street, between Second and Third.
Open daily 9:30–5:15. Free. Time: 25 minutes.

Return south along Second Street to Arch and turn west. On the north side stands the **Betsy Ross House (5)**. No book devoted to Old Philadelphia should fail to include this quaint little brick town house, with its large gable roof, shed dormer window, and paneled shutters. Its popularity is second only to the Liberty Bell. More than 300,000 people from every state in the country visit the house each year, and during the bicentennial year that number will be greater.

The house has been generally accepted as the home of Betsy Ross (1752–1836), the seamstress who is credited with the design and making of the forerunner of the Stars and Stripes, the flag of the original thirteen states. Historians point out that if she did in fact live at No. 239, she must have rented the building, for the Pennsylvania deeds in City Hall show that Hannah Lithgow owned the house between 1775 and 1779, when Betsy was supposed to have lived there.

Betsy Ross—or, to give her full name, Elizabeth Griscom Ross Ashbourn Claypoole—was raised a Quaker, and learned her trade at Webster's, the leading upholstery establishment of colonial Philadelphia. After she married her first husband, John Ross, she became involved in the patriot cause and joined the Free Quakers, or "Fighting Quakers" (see page 55).

She was by all accounts a reputable, industrious woman, and with the assistance of her daughters, granddaughters, and nieces, she continued a family flagmaking and upholstery business from Revolutionary days until her sight began to fail in 1827. Her fame, according to historian Margaret Tinkcom, began in 1870 when her grandson read a paper before the Historical Society of Pennsylvania reporting the account given him in 1836 (when he was eleven) by eighty-four-year-old Betsy herself, of the making of the Stars and Stripes. According to him, a committee composed of George Washington, Robert Morris, and George Ross, had called on Betsy to discuss the making of the flag. George Ross, a delegate to the Continental Congress, was the uncle of John Ross, Betsy's husband, who had died in an accident in 1776 while guarding military stores on Philadelphia's waterfront. Whether or not she made the first flag, Betsy certainly did make pennants and ensigns for the State Navy Board and she was widely known for her skill with the needle.

We do not know for certain if she did live in this little old house. But whether she did or not, No. 239 is still a fascinating example of a small eighteenth-century Philadelphia house (built 1760) with a basement kitchen, winding stairs, sitting room, and bedrooms. It is full of furniture and fixtures of the period and is well worth visiting.

Continue west on Arch Street, crossing Third. Between Nos. 321 and 323 Arch Street is **Loxely Court**. Enter the iron gates to view an intriguing backwater of restored eighteenth-century houses. Here at No. 2, in the eighteenth century, lived the carpenter Benjamin Loxely, who worked on Independence Hall and Carpenters' Hall. The court's greatest claim to fame—if its residents can be believed—is that Benjamin Franklin flew his celebrated kite here, and that the key he tied to it was the original key to Loxely's house. No. 8 was a tavern until taken over by the Methodists in 1768 before they moved to Old St. George's (see page 50).

Cross over Arch Street to the south side and you will find the **Arch Street Friends Meeting House (6)**. A long, low two-story building of typically plain design, this is a large and very famous Quaker meetinghouse. Its gateway, always left invitingly open during services, has impelled many a traveler to look in and join the congregation — the men on one side and women on the other. The English artist Eyre Crowe, who visited Philadelphia with Thackeray in 1853, was impressed by the degree of devotion he found there. Not a soul moved or turned to look as he tiptoed over the creaking boards to find a seat. It was built on a site granted to the Society of Friends by William Penn, but that had been used as a burial ground for about a hundred years. The meetinghouse was designed by Owen Biddle and erected in 1804.

Arch Street Friends Meeting House

Between Third and Fourth on Arch Street. Open daily 10:00–4:00. Exhibit Room displays interesting collection of memorabilia related to Quaker life. Dioramas depict main events of the life and achievements of William Penn. Free. Time: 25 minutes.

46

Quaker architects did not lavish a great deal of attention on their buildings. For the most part they were plain to the point of severity. The simple lines of this meetinghouse (still used for the Society of Friends' yearly meetings) were a reaction against what they felt to be unnecessary pomp and circumstance in following their humanist interpretation of Christianity.

Old First Reformed Church

151 North Fourth Street (southeastern corner of Fourth and Race). Call WA 2-7685 for times open. Youth hostel facilities for back-packing foreign and American students during summer. Time: 15 minutes.

If you have the time, recross Arch Street and continue north on Fourth to the **Old First Reformed Church (7)** of the United Church of Christ, one of the more recent church restorations in the Old City. There is an interesting story attached to it.

This simple church, originally the Mother Church of several German Reformed congregations, was founded in 1727, and the third building to occupy the site was abandoned in 1882. By that time, the neighborhood, originally German-speaking, had become a rundown business district. The church building itself became a paint factory and was abandoned in its turn. In 1959, the church building itself was again acquired. Years of accumulated debris and additions to the interior by the owner of the paint factory were removed, and the glories of the old church were once more revealed. As restoration work progressed in Society Hill and Independence Park, the nucleus of a new congregation returned.

The restored Old First Reformed Church is much more than a shrine, however. Besides the regular church services, there are recreational programs for neighborhood children, prison support, and services for veterans. The hearty German pioneers of Old Philadelphia would be as proud as ever of their church today.

Old St. George's

Southeast corner of New and North Fourth streets; one block north of Race. Open daily 10:00 – 4:00. Free guided tours. Time: 25 minutes.

Continue up North Fourth Street, beyond the Benjamin Franklin Bridge approach, to **Old St. George's Methodist Church (8)**, often called the "cradle of Methodism" in the New World and well worth visiting. Methodism in America has a colorful and exciting history, and a great deal of it seems to have taken place around this plain old Colonial church, fortunately saved from destruction. In 1921 the planners of the Benjamin Franklin Bridge sought a right-of-way over the ground on which the church was built. Being in the path of progress, it looked as if the historic old church had to go. Through the tenacity of Bishop Thomas Neely, the plans were altered to bypass the church by fourteen feet. The street had to be lowered, however, and the church now stands several feet above it.

Here Philadelphia's Methodists listened to the famous itinerant preachers sent to America by John Wesley. Captain Thomas Webb was certainly the most colorful of these. He came to America in 1755 as a quartermaster under General Braddock. He lost his right eye and almost his life at the siege of Louisburg in 1775. Thereafter, Captain Webb preached in his old uniform with his sword lying across the Bible, thumping the pulpit and threatening unrepentant souls with eternal damnation.

The old church is equally rich in historical associations involving the struggle for independence. When Washington was facing defeat at Valley Forge in 1777, he appealed to Robert Morris to send him $50,000 to feed and pay his ragged, starving army. Morris secured the money for him, having supposedly derived strength for the task from an all-night prayer meeting in St. George's Methodist Church.

Be sure not to miss the adjoining museum of the Methodist Historical Society, which contains old church silver, saddlebags used by itinerant circuit riders, and memorabilia of every kind, including the Bible and spectacles of Bishop Francis Asbury, leader of American Methodism.

As you leave, pause briefly at **St. Augustine's Catholic Church (★)** opposite. The present building is a reconstruction of the original church, which was destroyed in the anti-Catholic riots of 1844.

You may also wish to visit the **United States Mint (★)**. Go over to Fifth Street and then south to Race Street. Cross Race Street and you will see the entrance on the east side of Fifth. Open daily 9:00–3:30, except Saturdays, Sundays, and holidays. Free. Time: allow 45 minutes.

The Mint tour, self-guided and audiovisual, explains what is involved in making nickels, dimes, and quarters. There is a museum, too, calculated to drive any coin collector crazy. Note the Indian Head penny of 1836. You may be interested to learn that the model was *not* an Indian maid but twelve-year-old Sarah Longacre, daughter of James Barton Longacre, then chief engraver. When a visiting Indian chief placed a war bonnet on her head, a quick sketch was made by an unknown artist. It won the first prize of $1,000 for the design of the new one-cent piece.

Christ Church Burial Ground

Fifth and Arch streets. Open daily 9:00–4:00.
Time: 15 minutes.

Opposite the Mint and facing Independence Mall is **Christ Church Burial Ground (9)**, a hallowed spot in which time seems to have stood still. The grave of Benjamin Franklin can be seen through a special grating. Next to the patriarch and his combative wife, Deborah, lie various descendants and relatives. One pathetically small marker is for Francis Franklin, the son of Benjamin and Deborah, who died in 1736 at the age of four.

Within the burial ground itself are the weathered stones marking the last resting places of so many men, celebrated and respected in their time, whose names we will encounter again and again on our walks. Among them: John Dunlap, printer of the Declaration of Independence; Dr. John Kearsley, architect of Christ Church; Samuel Powel, an early mayor of Philadelphia; Thomas Willing, delegate to the Continental Congress and president of the First Bank of the United States; Francis Hopkinson, composer and signer of the Declaration of Independence; Captain Richard Budden, who brought both the Liberty Bell and the Christ Church bells from England; Dr. Philip Syng Physick, the father of American surgery; Dr. Benjamin Rush, physician and signer of the Declaration of Independence; Dr. Thomas Bond, a founder, with Benjamin Franklin, of the Pennsylvania Hospital; and many others.

Free Quaker Meetinghouse

Southwest corner, Fifth and Arch streets. Open daily 10:00 – 4:00; Sundays 12:00 – 4:00 from Memorial Day to Labor Day. Closed Mondays. Free guided tours. Time: 15 minutes.

Opposite the Christ Church Burial Ground on Independence Mall is the **Free Quaker Meetinghouse (10)**, our last point of interest on Walk 2. After years of neglect, the building was restored to the design of its founder, Samuel Wetherill (1736–1816), one of the original leaders of the Free ("Fighting") Quakers. The meetinghouse is now a museum devoted to the history of the group who, braving the wrath of fellow Friends, broke away to fight the British, and who built their own place of worship.

When the Revolutionary storm clouds gathered, the Society of Friends, long known for its opposition to force as a means of settling arguments between both people and nations, refused to join the cause of Independence. Although they denounced the actions of George III, they could not agree to armed rebellion. Some Quakers became supporters of the British and others joined the American cause. The Friends, however, disowned both groups. Those interested should read S. Weir Mitchell's novel *Hugh Wynne: Free Quaker* (1897), a powerful story of these events.

The Free Quakers erected their meetinghouse in 1783, and a marble tablet inserted in the north front reads:

> *By General Subscription*
> *For the Free Quakers, erected,*
> *In the year of our Lord, 1783,*
> *Of the Empire 8.*

"The Empire 8" apparently was a reference to the eighth year of "our country destined to be the great empire over all this world."

There were about a hundred members of the Free Quakers. Their leaders included Thomas Mifflin, signer of the Constitution and a general of the Revolutionary army; Samuel Wetherill, founder of the first manufacturing company for white lead in America (1762) and former Clerk of Meeting to the Society of Friends; Clement Biddle, colonel in the Revolutionary army and quartermaster; Lydia Darragh, whose revelation of a British plot overheard in her home saved Washington from an ambush at Whitemarsh; and Betsy Ross (then Elizabeth Griscom), who persisted in making flags for Congress, and was "read out of Meeting," as was Lydia Darragh after her courageous deed.

The Free Quaker Meetinghouse, like other Quaker meetinghouses, is very unlike the conventional Anglican or Episcopal churches of colonial times. There are no stained glass windows, beautiful candelabra, carved woodwork, or pulpits. Quakers felt that such objects, as well as music, distracted from their worship.

All these associations certainly helped me interpret the "no nonsense" of the Quakers, free or otherwise, in my drawing. Feeling I had overdone it, I added the gossiping squirrels being overheard by a typical Philadelphian.

We return to our starting point by way of Independence Mall, Pennsylvania's contribution to the creation of the Independence National Historic Park.

Walk 3
Society Hill

DISTANCE: 2 miles. TIME: one whole day of 5 to 6 hours, including a half-hour break for a sandwich lunch in Head House Square. If not possible, 2 to 3 hours, depending on how many of the mansions and churches are visited and how much time is spent in each.

Directly south of Independence Square, Society Hill, together with Southwark, constitutes the oldest residential area in the city; it was settled in the seventeenth century. Many mansions were built by citizens of wealth and, while Philadelphia was the capital of the United States (1790 – 1800), many political leaders and foreign notables lived in this area.

Society Hill takes its name from the Free Society of Traders, a short-lived British corporation that invested in William Penn's new colony and was granted land on and around the hill at the foot of Pine Street near the Delaware River. Long after the society had wound up its affairs and even though the hill had been almost leveled after the Revolution, the area continued to be called Society Hill.

After 1800, the city spread rapidly westward, but until well into the twentieth century many of the old houses continued to be occupied by descendants of the original families. After World War I, however, the once elegant resi-dential area began to run down. The historic mansions became tenements and workshops. By the middle of the twentieth century Society Hill was rapidly becoming a slum.

By the 1950s, the Philadelphia Redevelopment Authority, the City Historical Commission, the City Planning Commission, and other federal, civic, and private agencies set to work. Society Hill was reborn. Significant historic structures were identified, surveyed, and acquired by the city. These properties were then sold to anyone who would undertake proper restoration. The other buildings were demolished, and the cleared lots made available for housing of approved contemporary design.

Society Hill has many notable churches from the colonial period. Cosmopolitan and affluent eighteenth-century Philadelphia was a city with churches of all denominations. "I shall not usurp the right of any," Penn proclaimed, "or oppress his person." There are many notable mansions, too, some restored with original furnishings and open to the public as museums. But for the most part, Society Hill is hundreds of houses restored to their former grandeur and lived in by ordinary people; a "living, breathing example," wrote Nathaniel Burt, "of what a city can do for itself."

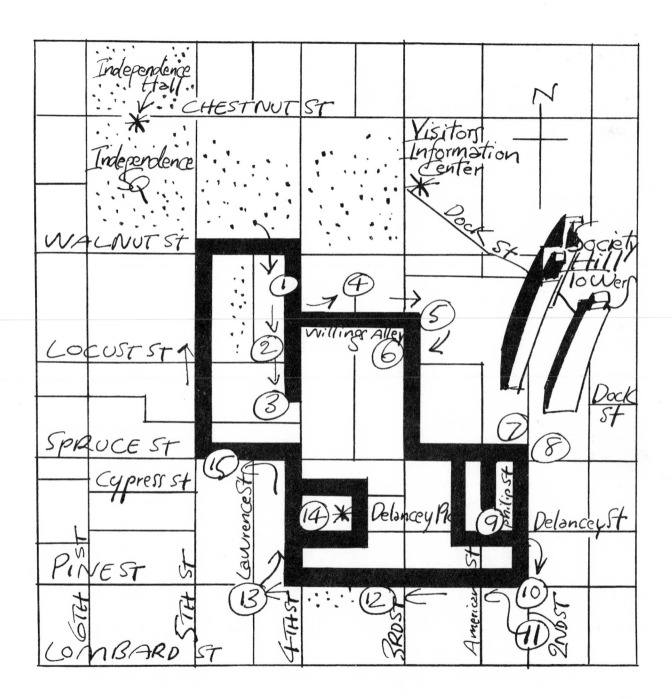

Independence Hall

CHESTNUT ST

Independence Sq

Visitors Information Center

N

Dock St

Society Hill Tower

WALNUT ST

1

4

5

LOCUST ST

2

Willings Alley

6

3

Dock St

7

8

SPRUCE ST

15

Cypress St

14

Delancey Pl

9

Philip St

Delancey St

PINE ST

Lawrence St

13

4TH ST

12

3RD ST

American St

10

2ND ST

5TH ST

6TH ST

LOMBARD ST

11

The Philadelphia Contributionship

212 South Fourth Street. Open daily, Monday through Friday, 9:00–4:00. Free. Time: 30 minutes.

Begin this walk on the south side of Independence Square, walking east on Walnut Street. Turn right on Fourth and continue south to the **Philadelphia Contributionship for the Insurance of Houses from Loss by Fire (1)**, at No. 212, head office of the oldest fire insurance company in America. The house itself was designed by Thomas Ustick Walter and was erected in 1836. It features elements of the Greek Revival style, although some of these have been removed.

Founded in 1752, The Philadelphia Contributionship itself is one of those many institutions that trace their origins to the versatile ingenuity of Benjamin Franklin. Fire had become a familiar and tragic problem. The trouble lay partly in the high inflammability of the eighteenth-century American town house, built around a shell of brick and stone but generously fitted out with wooden floors, windows, and stairs.

Fires were fought by volunteer citizen brigades equipped with little more than buckets and ladders. In 1736 Franklin helped found a fire-fighting system similar to that of London, where the insurance companies were responsible for both fighting fires and paying for damage and loss.

The Contributionship, followed by the Mutual Assurance Company (1784) and the Insurance Company of North America (1792), maintained its own brigades of men trained to put out fires in the houses of the insured. Identification of such houses was necessary, and a firemark was therefore provided. Each company had its own distinctive emblem (see Appendix, pages 147 – 148). That of the Contributionship was the hand-in-hand designed by the silversmith, Philip Syng, a director of the company, and cast by John Stow.

The historical mood is immediately apparent upon entry; when you sign the guest book with a quill pen, you receive one as a souvenir. Begin your tour on the fourth floor, where you will find an insurance office as it would have been before 1900. On the second floor is the board room, elegantly furnished with mahogany cane-seated chairs. There are also fine portraits and candelabra. The museum on the first floor has a fascinating collection of early fire-fighting equipment.

The Shippen-Wistar House

Southwest corner of Fourth and Locust streets. Not open to the public.

Leaving the treasures of the Philadelphia Contributionship, we continue south to Locust Street, which enters Fourth from the right. Directly opposite, on the corner, is the **Shippen-Wistar House (2),** one of the most historic houses in Society Hill, dating from about 1750 and now occupied by the Mutual Assurance Company for Insuring Houses from Loss by Fire.

A typical wealthy Philadelphian's home of the late eighteenth and early nineteenth century, this famous old house with its well-proportioned exterior and richly ornamental cast-iron railings has been restored with appropriate period furniture and memorabilia.

The house was occupied by a succession of colorful personalities. The first was its builder, Dr. William Shippen, Sr. (1712 – 1801), celebrated physician and delegate to the Continental Congresses of 1778 and 1779. It was later occupied by his son, Dr. William Shippen, Jr. (1736–1808), a physician, professor of anatomy and surgery at the College of Philadelphia, and director general of the Medical Service of the Continental army. He was the object of much public controversy because of his "body-snatching" activities. He was one of the first to use dead bodies for dissection in his classes. Sometimes he received the bodies of executed criminals but sometimes—he admitted the charge—he stole them from Potter's Field, smuggling them—in the dead of night, naturally—into the house through the arched gate shown at the far right of my picture. The practice was continued by an even more celebrated physician who occupied the house in 1798. This was Dr. Caspar Wistar (1761–1818), also a professor of anatomy at the University of Pennsylvania, a physician in Pennsylvania Hospital, and author of the first anatomical textbook in the United States. Dr. Wistar's famous Saturday night parties for leading scientists, statesmen, and visiting scholars established a continuing Philadelphia tradition. He succeeded Thomas Jefferson as president of the American Philosophical Society, and his memory is preserved by the Wistar Parties, which are given by members to perpetuate his wit and hospitality.

Old St. Mary's

252 South Fourth Street. Open daily 8:00 Mass only; Sundays 9:00–12:00. Time: 25 minutes.

Continue for a few steps on Fourth Street and you will come to **Old St. Mary's Roman Catholic Church (3)**, founded in 1763 and the principal Catholic church in Philadelphia during the Revolutionary period. A plain exterior conceals a richly ornamental interior with an elaborate high altar and Victorian Crucifixion window. In the peaceful cemetery behind, many prominent American Catholics are buried, including Thomas Fitzsimmons, delegate to the Constitutional Convention; Commodore John Barry, "Father of the American Navy"; Stephen Moylan, aide-de-camp to Washington; Mathew Carey, leading Philadelphia publisher; and Michael Bouvier, ancestor of Jacqueline Bouvier Kennedy Onassis.

Old St. Joseph's

Willing's Alley, between Third and Fourth streets. Open daily 6:30 – 6:00. Time: 15 minutes.

Cross Fourth and retrace your steps north, to Willing's Alley. Turn right and walk halfway down until you see the arched doorway of **Old St. Joseph's Roman Catholic Church (4)**, hidden away behind an iron gate. Enter and cross the inner courtyard to the church. Although Pennsylvania allowed Catholics to worship publicly, anti-Catholic feelings ran high on occasion, especially during the colonial wars with France. Hence the iron gate and concealed site of the little church.

The first church was built in 1733, enlarged in 1821, and finally rebuilt in 1838. It was always a refuge for the poor and the dispossessed; the socially prominent Catholic families preferred St. Mary's. The original congregation was composed primarily of Irish and German artisans and servants.

But there were many others besides Irish and Germans in the early congregations. Among them were the unfortunate Acadians, expelled during the Seven Years' War from Grand Pré, Acadia (in what is now Nova Scotia), celebrated in Longfellow's epic poem *Evangeline*. Fifteen thousand Acadians arrived in Philadelphia in 1755 and were housed in huts on Pine Street between Fifth and Sixth. In Longfellow's poem, Evangeline found her Acadian lover Gabriel in a Philadelphia almshouse. The poet visited the city in 1824, saw the Quaker Almshouse (now demolished) next door to St. Joseph's, which was used to accommodate the Acadians, and thought it appropriate as the meeting place of the ill-starred lovers. Here also they died and were buried in "the little Catholic churchyard" of Holy Trinity Catholic Church (See Walk 6, pages 122–123).

Another exile was Joseph Bonaparte (1768 – 1844), the elder brother of Napoleon. The ex-king of Naples and Spain arrived in the United States in 1815 and remained in Philadelphia for many years, renting No. 260 South Ninth Street (see Walk 6, pages 124–141) until he moved to his estate in New Jersey. Louis Philippe lived nearby at Fourth Street and Locust (1796 – 1800) as did Talleyrand on South Second Street (1794 – 1796) and many other earlier French exiles.

Instead of using the exit onto Walnut Street, retrace your steps through the courtyard and leave the church by Willing's Alley, walking east toward the river. Before you, on Third Street, is the facade of Old St. Paul's our next port of call.

Old St. Paul's

225 South Third Street. Open Monday through Friday, 9:00–4:45. Time: 15 minutes. Headquarters of the Episcopal Community Services of Pennsylvania.

Old St. Paul's Church (5), built in 1761, was remodeled in 1830 in something of a Greek Revival style by William Strickland. It was founded in 1760 to absorb the radical zeal of the Reverend William McClenachan, assistant to the rector of Christ Church and an outspoken young clergyman who had disturbed the tranquility of that congregation by advocating the separation of church and state.

Some of the finest of its treasures have been removed to other churches. The sounding board, with a pair of life-sized angels carved by William Rush, which hung above the pulpit, is now at St. Peter's and the sacramental silver is at the new St. Paul's at Fifteenth and Porter streets. There is, however, a baptismal font and a bishop's chair that date back to the seventeenth century.

During the British occupation of Philadelphia the church was converted into a hospital. It was filled with the wounded of both armies after the Battle of Germantown. Large pits were dug in and around the church in which the dead were thrown—without coffins. In the graveyard proper lie many Philadelphians of the period: prominent merchants, sea captains, soldiers of the Revolutionary War, doctors, lawyers, and politicians. Among the more famous are the Reverend William McClenachan himself; General Thomas Proctor, of Whisky Rebellion fame; and Edwin Forrest (1806 – 1872), the great tragedian whose long-standing feud with the English actor William Macready led to the Astor Place Riot (a demonstration against Macready by Forrest partisans) in New York in 1849, in which thirty people lost their lives.

Continue south on the east side of Third and look across at the row of fine old mansions **(6)**. Some of these are privately owned; others are used as offices. Walk south, starting from right to left.

Mansion Block, South Third Street

No. 232: Bishop Stevens House. Built 1843–1846 by Dr. Charles Willing, member of the old Philadelphia family, and occupied by him 1846–1855; then by Frederick Vincent, gentleman, 1855–1862. Both this and No. 234 are now used as the offices of the Episcopal Community Services. Note the cast-iron balcony of striking design, using the motif of a Roman griffin, a fabled creature with an eagle's head and wings and a lion's body.

No. 234: Also built at the same time, has a matching cast-iron balcony with the motif of a hunting dog. This house passed through several hands before it settled down first as the Merchants' Club, 1873–1878; and then as the Mercantile Club, 1878–1895.

No. 236: Built in 1824 by master bricklayer Amos Atkinson. By 1964, "it looked like a ninth-rate boarding house." Its present owners have restored the facade to its original Federal elegance. The inside, however, is strictly California style, complete with pool.

No. 238: Built in 1823 for Charles Robb and David Winebrener, merchant tailors, the house was then occupied by Horace Rowley, master plumber, followed by Isaiah Canby, grocer. Between 1876 and 1881, the young Philadelphia architect Wilson Eyre gave it a new facade; it was later an office for another well-known architect of the era, Frank Miles Day, 1880–1890. Unfortunately, Eyre's facade was removed during restoration in 1963–1964.

No. 240: Built 1829–1936 and occupied by Henry White, merchant; then Charles S. Boker, the banker who was thought to have wrecked

— but had actually saved — the Girard Bank from insolvency after the Panic of 1837. American Legion Post 132 is the present owner.

No. 242: The oldest part of this historic house dates back to 1766. John Penn, grandson of William and last colonial governor of Pennsylvania, lived here 1766–1771. Benjamin Chew, the last colonial chief justice of Pennsylvania, owned the house from 1771 to 1810. From 1778 to 1780 Juan de Miralles, the first Spanish diplomatic representative to the United States,

lived there, as did his successor, Francisco Rondon, who lent it to Washington during the winter of 1781–1782. It is now the home of Mr. and Mrs. Albert M. Greenfield, Jr.

No. 244: Powel House. Built 1765, and the home of Samuel Powel, the last colonial mayor of Philadelphia and the first after Independence. Samuel's wife, Elizabeth, was the daughter of Thomas Willing, partner of banker Robert Morris, who financed the Revolution. Many celebrated statesmen, including Washington

and John Adams, enjoyed the Powels' legendary hospitality.

The Powel House is open Tuesday through Saturday 10:00–5:00; Sundays 1:00–5:00; it closes at 4:00 in winter. Also open for special Monday holidays. Adults $1.00; children 25 cents. Time: at least 45 minutes for both house and garden. It is worthwhile to go inside and take the guided tour. You will learn the dramatic story of how this historic old mansion was saved from demolition.

Perelman Antique Toy Museum

270 South Second Street. Open daily 9:30–5:00. Admission: Adults $1.00; children under 14, 55 cents; Service people 55 cents. Time: 25 minutes.

Continue south on Third. Note the variety of fine Colonial, post-Revolutionary, and Greek Revival ironwork on this street: handrails and newel posts with footscrapers built in or set apart in white marble blocks flush with the sidewalk. (See pages 142–144 for some typical designs.) Make a left turn at Spruce Street and left again on Second. Immediately to your left, overshadowed by the three skyscraper blocks known as Society Hill Towers, is the **Perelman Antique Toy Museum (7)**.

Located in the restored house of the sea captain James Abercrombie, the museum is devoted entirely to American toys of the Victorian era. It is fascinating for the variety and quality of the folk art so ingeniously displayed. There are 2,000 tin or cast-iron toys to be seen, as well as the world's largest collection of mechanical banks—in themselves a graphic rev-

elation of the Quaker and Victorian obsession with saving. One of the automated toys shows President Ulysses S. Grant seated in a chair, smoking a big black cigar and leisurely turning his head to puff out the smoke. There are massed displays of a collection devoted to stagecoaches, the United States Cavalry, and Conestoga wagons.

A few steps from the museum, just across Second Street on Spruce, is a picturesque Colonial inn, **A Man Full of Trouble (8)**, a restoration of what one can well imagine must have been a colorful haunt. In those days, an inn or tavern was licensed to provide lodging for travelers and to serve meals and beverages to both strangers and local customers. Philadelphia was a port of entry for a rising tide of immigrants and travelers. Situated on one of its busiest streets, the inn did a thriving business until 1884.

Colonel Blaithwaite Jones, the commander of the Delaware River defenses against the British forces, was one early owner. Widow Smallwood, who ran the place as a "genteel establishment" for thirty years, was another.

The inn, together with the adjacent Paschall House, was originally built in 1759. Both were faced with certain demolition in 1960 because of their slanting walls and weakened foundations, but the Knauer Foundation stepped in to preserve them. The inn is the last of a score of eighteenth-century inns once a familiar sight throughout the old city.

Because of its character, the inn affords a very different look at the past from what we have seen so far. Here we are confronted by Philadelphia's seafaring history, and the

Early mechanical bank circa 1867.

A Man Full of Trouble Inn

125-127 Spruce Street. Open daily except Mondays. Summer: 1:30 – 4:00; winter: 1:00 – 4:00. Adults 50 cents; children over ten 25 cents; children under ten free. Last tour at 3:30.

sailors, chandlers, and dockers who patronized the inn. The tiny rooms with low ceilings resemble the cabins of an eighteenth-century ship.

The intimate barroom, with its early American furniture, pewter tankards and platters, is particularly inviting. The large basement kitchen, with the tunnel that led to Little Dock Creek, has many of its original fixtures. These were discovered when the cellars were excavated. Upstairs there are musket slots on the landings for defending the inn against attack, a spacious "Captain's Room" facing the river, and a small attic for seamen.

Barclay-Rhoads House

305 Delancey Street. Not open to the public.

We are now on our way to Head House and Second Street Market, but this diversion won't take longer than 15 minutes. Proceed west on Spruce past Second Street. Note the many restored houses. No. 217, for example, is the Davis-Lennox House, built in 1759 by James Davis, master carpenter and officer of the Carpenters' Company. In 1784 it was enlarged by David Lennox, soldier, banker, and diplomat. Turn left at Philip Street and wander along its cobblestones. This old street, with adjacent American Street, is another picturesque section of Society Hill. Both are lined with old houses, which, although smaller and more modest, seem quite authentic.

As you emerge from Philip Street into Delancey, note the little house on the corner. This is the **Barclay-Rhoads House (9)**, built in 1758 for Alexander Barclay, comptroller of the Port of Philadelphia, 1750–1751. It is a typical two-and-a-half-story Colonial town house with gable roof, shed dormer, paneled shutters and door, and traditional Germantown "hood" over the entrance and windows. Its builder, Samuel Rhoads (1711–1784), was a prominent member of the Carpenters' Company, a delegate to the First Continental Congress, and the mayor of Philadelphia in 1774. He also built Franklin's house and much of Pennsylvania Hospital.

Stroll west up Delancey Street and turn right into American Street. Then retrace your steps via this street or Philip Street and continue east on Delancey until you come to Second. Turn right at Second and proceed south to **Head House Square (10)** and **Second Street Market (11)**.

Head House Square

This historic square, originally built in 1740–1811 and restored in 1957–1966, provides a good idea of what eighteenth-century Philadelphia must have been like. Today, beautifully restored with shops, restaurants, an ice-cream parlor, and a drugstore, the square has a unique atmosphere. At the Pine Street end two buildings stand out: **Head House**, built in 1803 as an office and residence for the Market Master, who collected fees, tested the quality of goods, and policed the market, is a handsome boxlike building graced by a cupola and weathervane. The clock built by Isaiah Lukens and installed in 1819 is once again in good working order. Head House is flanked on each side by rows of substantial houses from the eighteenth and early nineteenth centuries.

Across the street on the southeast corner of Lombard (not included in my picture or map) is **Ross House**. Built in 1780, it is a notable example of a large Philadelphia town house, and one that Washington is said to have frequented. On the southwest corner is Head House Tavern, a pleasant reconstruction of an eighteenth-century ale house with furnishings typical of the period.

Around the square lived merchants, sea captains, bakers, blacksmiths, and cabinetmakers; the latter had shops fronting on the square. That some enjoyed a standard of living far more cultivated than has been generally thought is indicated by the excavations of wells and privies in 1973–1974 by a team of urban archaeologists led by the indefatigable Dr. Barbara Liggett. A startling lode of artifacts was uncovered, including examples of rare English porcelain never before found in Philadelphia.

Old Second Street Market

Just behind Head House are the arcades of restored **Second Street Market**, built in 1745 and restored in 1962–1963. The old market had been city property before the Revolution and a few stalls were still occupied in the 1950s. But it looked then as though its days were numbered; in fact, a demolition firm had already started to tear down some sheds. At the last moment Mayor Richardson Dilworth intervened, and the only surviving colonial marketplace in the city was saved. That was in 1956.

Now, in summer, the market is like a country fair; artists and craftsmen set up stalls on weekends, and there are free concerts and flea markets.

As you are now halfway through the walk, you may find, as I did, that the square offers facilities that make it a natural point at which to break off for lunch. I found the Lautrec, Head House Tavern, and the ice-cream parlor all agreeable places; although the Lautrec is perhaps preferable for dinner.

St. Peter's

Third and Pine streets. Open Monday through Friday 9:00 – 4:00. Visitors must be accompanied by the sexton, who can be found at the parish house opposite the church, No. 313 Pine Street. Telephone: WA 5-5968. Time: 25 minutes; add another 25 if you are a tombstone buff.

Go west on Pine Street to Third. Here, half hidden among a row of giant elms, is one of the finest Colonial churches in the United States, **St. Peter's Protestant Episcopal Church (12)**. It was built between 1761 and 1763 in a rectangular design by Robert Smith on land given by Thomas and Richard Penn.

Surrounded by its old overgrown churchyard, St. Peter's is a picturesque focal point in itself. The most interesting part of the exterior is the tall, slim belfry tower, six stories high and surmounted by a narrow wooden steeple added in 1842. Inside, one is reminded of Christ Church, but St. Peter's is perhaps even more beautiful in its pristine dignity, enhanced by the multicolored hues of the stained glass windows. An unusual feature is the double-ended seating plan: an altar at the east end for one part of the service and a wineglass pulpit for the sermon at the west end. The rows of cedar box pews painted white, where Washington sat with his friend Samuel Powel, complete the perfect picture of gracious churchgoing.

Note the house on the northwest corner of Pine and Third Street (on the far right of my picture). For almost two years this was the home of Thaddeus Kosciusko (1746–1817), the Polish soldier and statesman who first came to America in 1776 to fight under Washington in the Revolutionary army. It was an experience that must have shaped his democratic ideas, and in 1793 he returned to Poland to lead an unsuccessful uprising against Russia. He was captured and imprisoned, but Czar Paul freed him in 1796 and he returned to America and lived in Philadelphia. Kosciusko was one of the few foreign volunteers who distinguished themselves in the War for Independence, and he rose to the rank of general of the engineers.

79

Congress granted him a pension and land, but he returned again to fight for Polish independence in 1798 and was again defeated. The unlucky patriot retired in despair to Switzerland, where he died.

In the churchyard, it is easy to forget time and spend all afternoon looking at tombstones, many of great historical interest. Among the oldest are the graves of Benjamin Chew, Chief Justice of Pennsylvania; and Dr. William Shippen, Sr., both of whose houses we passed earlier. We enter the Federal period with the tombstone of Commodore Stephen Decatur (1779–1820), the naval hero whose death as the result of a dual with his lifelong enemy, Commodore James Barron, terminated a career of reckless courage and stubborn patriotism. In 1804 Jefferson had sent the tiny American navy, with the United States Marines aboard, "to the shores of Tripoli" to settle once and for all the matter of paying tribute to the piratical Barbary states. In this and other campaigns Decatur distinguished himself over a period of years. His grave is marked by a tall, grooved Doric column topped by an appropriately militant American eagle.

Note also the grave of Charles Willson Peale, portrait painter extraordinary and founder of the celebrated Peale's Museum, defined as the first modern museum because it sought not only to assist the scholar but to instruct the layman.

Among the ivy at the east front is the grave of another remarkable American, the Philadelphia patrician, Nicholas Biddle (1786–1844), man of letters, lawyer, diplomat, and banker—in that order. As a young man he was a leading light in America's literary world. He prepared the journals of Lewis and Clark for publication, and he advocated a system of

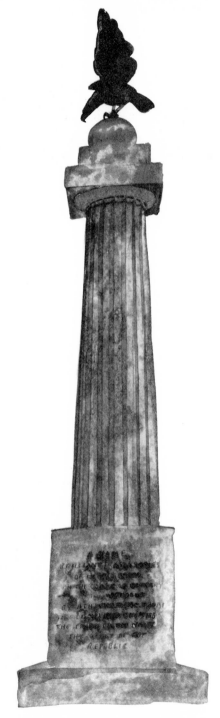

Grave of Stephen Decatur (1779–1820), naval hero.

Grave of Charles Willson Peale (1741–1827), painter.

popular education well ahead of the time.

Another grave that invites reflection is that of the Reverend Jacob Duché. He had risen to prominence as rector of Christ Church and St. Peter's, and his support of the First Continental Congress before the Revolution set him high in public esteem. After Valley Forge he gave up hope for the revolutionary cause and urged Washington to have the Declaration of Independence annulled by Congress and to make the best possible terms with the British.

Everyone turned against him, and he left America for England. He could not forget Philadelphia, however, and when the war was over he returned, hoping for his old post; but this had already been filled by the Reverend William White, and there was no place for Duché. Previous popularity, influential connections, old friends—nothing made any difference. He lingered on until near the end of the eighteenth century, when he died—unhappy, alone, and unforgiven.

Grave of Nicholas Biddle (1786–1844), man of letters, diplomat, and financier.

81

Old Pine Street Church

412 Pine Street. Open Monday through Friday 1:00–5:00. Time: 25 minutes; add another 25 for examining tombstones. Concerts every Sunday at 4:30. Call WA 5-8051 for program.

Across Fourth Street—the very next block, in fact—is **Old Pine Street Presbyterian Church (13)** or, to give its full name, the Third Scots and Mariners Presbyterian Church, but affectionately nicknamed "Old Pine" by local residents. Like St. Peter's, it is surrounded on all sides by a peaceful old graveyard where many famous Philadelphians are buried.

Old Pine, built 1767–1768, is the only Presbyterian church among the eight colonial churches still standing in the city. Its architect was Robert Smith, the designer of St. Peter's. The original building is said to have been simpler, rather like Old St. Paul's, but extensive alterations were made in 1837. The roof was raised and an imposing Greek Revival front added. This gave the church a ground floor which could be used for a Sunday school (now a community nursery), and a second floor for an auditorium. The original character of the church disappeared: Corinthian columns grouped together in pairs transformed it into a handsome classic temple.

Entering by the portico or from an entrance at street level, you will find that the interior itself has a beguiling intimacy, making it ideal for the concerts on Sunday afternoons. These start early in September, continue through the winter, and include a revival of traditional evensong presented by Franklin Zimmerman of the Pennsylvania Pro Musica. Devotional music of early masters such as Palestrina is performed admirably.

Like most Presbyterian churches, Old Pine has had more than its share of involvement with the struggle for independence. Some sixty members of its congregation fought with the Revolutionary army, thirty-five serving as officers. Its first pastor, the militant George Duffield, appears to have set the pace. He was so

Grave of Colonel William Linnard, Revolutionary War hero.

83

active that the British set a price on his head. After war was declared against England, he became chaplain of the First Continental Congress and the Pennsylvania militia. His church, well known for its stand, became a target of vengeance when the British occupied Philadelphia in 1777. While the dandies of the army chatted amiably with the belles of Society Hill at St. Peter's, the pews of Old Pine were ripped out for firewood and the church used as a stable by the dragoons. Insult was added to injury when it was later used as a military hospital. A hundred unfortunate Hessians who died of their wounds lie buried in a common grave in the churchyard.

After the Revolution, Duffield's pastorship attracted an influential following. He was a close friend of John Adams's, who frequently attended the church to hear him preach. His hardheaded Christianity obviously had a strong appeal for the puritanical second president of the United States. Other prominent communicants included Benjamin Rush, the American physician who urged Thomas Paine to write *Common Sense*. Another medical man was Dr. William Shippen, Jr. Rush and Shippen were bitter enemies, and each had devoted followers who took up the arguments and accusations of their respective idols.

The graveyard rivals that of St. Peter's in its variety of ivy-wreathed tombstones, vaults, and monuments. The ground east and south of

Grave of William Hurrie, who rang the Liberty Bell proclaiming independence.

the church and the first row of graves on the west constitute the original burial ground. Among the graves is that of Colonel William Linnard, master carpenter, who placed the cannon at the mouth of Wissahickon and opened fire on the Hessians at the bloody Battle of Germantown.

Here also is the grave of William Hurrie, said to have rung the Liberty Bell in 1776 when the Declaration of Independence was proclaimed. Not far away lies General John Steele, aide-de-camp to Washington in New Jersey and field officer of the day when Lord Cornwallis surrendered at Yorktown on October 19, 1781. The great company of notables also includes David Rittenhouse, the celebrated mathematician and astronomer; Jared Ingersoll, attorney general of Pennsylvania and delegate to the Constitutional Convention in 1787; Colonel William Rush, custodian of the State House and officer in the Revolutionary army; and last but not least, Thomas Brainerd, one of Philadelphia's antislavery leaders and a founder of the Union Club on Broad Street. When Brainerd was buried the whole Union Club attended in a body.

Leaving Old Pine, walk north on Fourth Street, turn right down Delancey Street, and then walk left through Delancey Park. A few steps farther to Cypress Street will bring you back to Fourth Street and our next stop, the **Hill-Physick-Keith House (14)**.

Grave of General John Steele, aide-de-camp to Washington.

Hill-Physick-Keith House

321 South Fourth Street. Open Tuesday through Saturday 10:00–5:00; Sundays 1:00–5:00; Winter till 4:00. Open four special Monday holidays. Adults $1.00; children 25 cents. Telephone: WA 5-7866. Time: allow at least 30 minutes for both house and garden.

On the east side of Fourth, between Delancey and Cypress streets, stands **Hill-Physick-Keith House**, a mansion of exceptional interest. Built in 1786, this handsome freestanding house was restored in 1965 by the Annenberg Fund and given to the Philadelphia Society for the Preservation of Landmarks.

The house is graced with many of its original furnishings, supplemented by loans of French and American pieces from the Philadelphia Museum of Art. Its first owner, Henry Hill, was a successful wine merchant who liked to entertain lavishly. Benjamin Franklin was a good friend, and no doubt the many empty bottles found on the site of the patriarch's house once contained Hill's celebrated Madeira. But Hill was also a staunch patriot and contributed a substantial amount of money to buy food for Washington's army.

After 1790 the house was occupied by Dr. Philip Syng Physick, whose daring use of the latest gadgets—one was the stomach pump—enabled him to save many lives. Chief Justice Marshall was one of his patients. Among the gifts made to him in gratitude is a silver wine cooler (on view) given in 1831 when Dr. Physick brought the tall, gaunt chief justice through a successful operation for the removal of a painful gallstone. After the doctor's death in 1837, the house passed through various branches of the family to Mrs. Charles Penrose Keith. Be sure to visit the spacious garden laid out in the style popular during the Federal period.

Society Hill Synagogue

426 Spruce Street. Group visits are welcome if notice is given to Rabbi Ivan Caine at No. 418; telephone: WA 5-8768. Time: allow 20 minutes.

Continue on Fourth and turn left at Spruce. On your left is the massive stone and stucco **Society Hill Synagogue (15)**, a Greek Revival structure built in 1829 as the Spruce Street Baptist Church. It served as a church from 1830 to 1911, and is now the home of the Rumanian-American Congregation Oir Chodosh Agudas-Achim and the An Spak Thal School.

This large, chunky edifice has the distinction of being designed by Thomas Ustick Walter, whose work we previously encountered on Walk 1 and earlier on this Walk with the Philadelphia Contributionship house. He is thought to have designed the original church at the beginning of his career. Walter and his parents were prominent Baptists and he himself was baptized in the Schuylkill River on July 12, 1829, and on the same day was received into membership of the Spruce Street Baptist Church. In fact, the enlargement and new front for the church was his last commission before leaving the city in 1851 to work on the Capitol, Washington, D.C.

The Philadelphia-born Walter was the son of a master stonemason who had the stonework contract for the Second Bank of the United States. He was apprenticed to his father and, while working on the bank, his talent as a draftsman impressed the great William Strickland. He completed his apprenticeship and studied architecture at the Franklin Institute, where Strickland was the instructor. He designed many prominent buildings in Philadel-

phia and is credited with introducing the Egyptian style in the city. But his most typical work is neoclassical in style and his greatest design, Founders Hall of Girard College, is perhaps the prime example of the Greek Revival style in the United States.

Walter's design for Spruce Street Baptist Church is unusual for its generous use of consoles, or brackets. These are used in various forms and sizes to support cornices at the top and above the windows and front door. Note the huge pair supporting the cornice above the door. These are erect consoles of Greek style and based on those found on the North Door of the Erechtheum, Athens. The square corner towers were originally topped with attics and cupolas. Unfortunately, these were removed in 1911 when the building was adapted for use as a synagogue.

One cannot help but wonder why this ornate style impressed the zealous revivalist Baptists. Part of the answer is that during the Federal era *all* Americans thought Greek Revival the last word in modern taste. But the rediscovery of the classical was not just the point of departure for a new ideal of design, but the consequence of a new confidence felt by all religious groups, and with it the urge to sweep away the more Spartan simplicity of Georgian architecture.

Cross Spruce and turn right into Fifth Street; then proceed north across Locust to Walnut. This will bring you back to your starting point.

Walk 4
A Glimpse of Southwark

DISTANCE: 3 miles. TIME: at least 3 hours, depending on the length of your visit to Gloria Dei, or Old Swedes' Church.

Time can be saved by taking a Second Street bus south to Christian Street. Walk two blocks east to Old Swedes' Church. Start your tour there and end with the Mifflin Houses. To the southeast of the city lies Southwark, bounded on the north and south by Lombard and Carpenter streets, and on the east and west by Swanson and Sixth streets.

Southwark was founded in 1638 by Swedish settlers who called it Wicaco, its Indian name for almost a half century before the first British colonists founded Philadelphia. The original settlement was located on the banks of the Delaware around the area of Gloria Dei. Later, the borough spread north and west. By the middle of the eighteenth century it had become Southwark (pronounced south-work) after the London borough south of the Thames (pronounced suth-ark).

By this time Southwark had become the focus of the thriving commerce and bustling shipbuilding activity that made Philadelphia the biggest port of the colonies and of the youthful United States. The first United States Navy Yard was located a few blocks south of Old Swedes' Church. Here, as in London's Southwark, lived merchants, captains, shipwrights—all the craftsmen and tradesmen involved with the sea. Southwark can hardly be thought of as being other than a section of Philadelphia today, but it still possesses the aura of a seafaring community, and, therefore, much of its original personality.

Yet, old as it is, Southwark is the least known section of the city, partly because it is still undergoing the agonies of restoration and redevelopment. Quite frankly, much of it looks as though an atomic bomb had exploded over it, particularly around the area cleared for the Delaware Expressway (Interstate 95) between Front Street and the river. One day the expressway will doubtless be completed. Meanwhile, Southwark is quietly rejuvenating itself. Many of the oldest houses in the city are located here and although most have yet to be restored, many are already in the process, particularly in the neighborhood known as Queen Village, between Bainbridge and Fitzwater streets and Front and Second streets. For the visitor who passes through Southwark, first impressions may be unfavorable, but these are soon replaced by a growing appreciation of its historic past.

We begin at Head House Square, visited on Walk 3. Our starting point is Lombard and South Second streets.

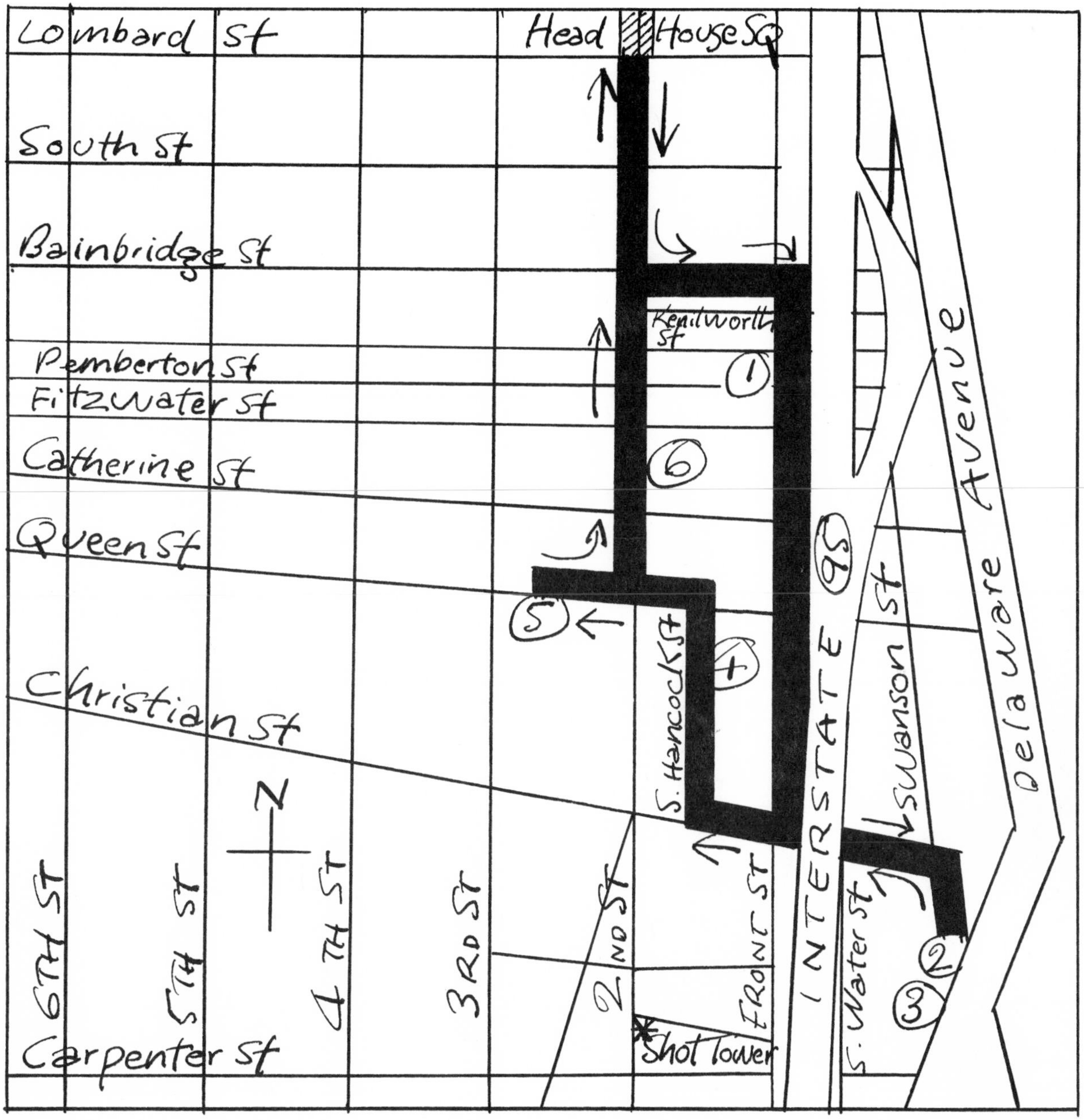

Lombard St | Head House Sq

South St

Bainbridge St

Kenilworth St

Pemberton St
Fitzwater St
Catherine St

Queen St

Christian St

Carpenter St

Interstate 95

Delaware Avenue

S. Swanson St

S. Water St

Front St

S. Hancock St

2nd St

3rd St

4th St

5th St

6th St

Shot Tower

N

① ② ③ ④ ⑤ ⑥

91

The Mifflin Houses

Pemberton Street. Houses are not open to
the public, although both garden and houses
can be viewed through the entrance gate.
Time: Allow 15 minutes.

Turn left at Bainbridge, then right at Front. Continue south on Front, passing Kenilworth and Pemberton streets. Between Pemberton and Fitzwater streets, Nos. 742, 744, and 746 constitute a unique group of historic houses known as Workman Place. Built in 1812, it is operated by the Octavia Hill Association as a low-cost housing project. Turn into Pemberton Street to view the **Mifflin Houses (1)**, of particular interest as they were built much earlier. The gable walls proclaim: ''GM 1748.'' GM means George Mifflin; and 1748, the year they were built. George Mifflin was the grandfather of General Thomas Mifflin, signer of the Constitution and builder of Fort Mifflin.

I wandered through the little iron gateway, reminded more than ever of Southwark, England, to eneer a tranquil courtyard where time seems to have stood still. Most of the tenants have lived here all their lives. Many are longshoremen who work along the Delaware.

93

Gloria Dei (Old Swedes') Church

Swanson and Christian streets. Open daily 9:00–5:00. Free guided tours. Call ahead if you are a large group. Telephone: DE 6-7080. Time: allow at least 30 minutes for your visit to a church of exceptional interest; more if you wish to browse in the churchyard.

Old Swedes in the Autumn

Retrace your steps to Front Street and continue south four blocks, turning east on Christian. Note the many old houses along the street. Turn right at Swanson and enter the gate of **Gloria Dei**, popularly known as **Old Swedes' Church (2)**, and now a national shrine.

The exquisite, toylike simplicity of this ancient church provides a poignant contrast to the modern world outside; one enters an oasis of complete tranquility. Work began on the church in 1698 and was completed in 1700. It was built in a traditional Swedish style by John Smart, John Brett, and John Harrison and is similar in design to Swedes' Church, Wilmington, Delaware.

The church is entered by a simple porch added in 1705 which, in itself, is beautiful indeed. The interior, with side balconies, has the feel of a much earlier period. Models of the ships that brought the first Swedish settlers to the shores of the New World hang from the ceiling. The heads of two worldly-looking angels, originally part of a ship's figurehead, hang under the organ.

It was fall when I made my visit. The old church sat serenely in the center of its graveyard, and the great trees shed their leaves, which lay in golden heaps on the tombstones of the great. Note the grave of Alexander Wilson (1766–1813), father of American ornithology, who begged that he be buried there. It was a silent, shady place, he said, where the birds would always come and sing over his grave.

Revolutionary Corner

Not far away is **Revolutionary Corner (3)** where eight of the most famous officers of Washington's army have found their last resting place. The Pennsylvania Chapter of the Daughters of Founders and Patriots of America brought the tombstones here after the demolition of Ronaldson's Cemetery in 1952. The eight officers are Brigadier General William Irving, Colonel Robert Rae,. Major James Moore, and Captains Abraham Parsons, Michael Marsons, James Peale, Thomas Taylor, and James F. Moore.

After you have recovered from the spell of Old Swedes' Church, leave by Swanson Street, turn left and continue on Christian until you come to **South Hancock Street (4)**. Proceed north about halfway toward Queen Street, and note the two tiny clapboard houses at Nos. 813 and 815. The houses were built in 1786 by Thomas Penrose, shipwright, and are the last of their type.

Visible behind the Penrose houses is a famous old landmark, the Shot Tower, which was the first in America. It was built by John Bishop and Thomas Sparks in 1807 as a do-it-yourself enterprise. Congress had stopped all imports from Europe, including shot. Bishop, a Quaker, withdrew from the partnership when the War of 1812 caused the Shot Tower's product to be used as munitions. It is now a city playground.

Wooden houses, 1786. South Hancock Street with Shot Tower.

97

St. Philip Neri Church

Queen Street between Second and Third streets. Masses: Sundays 6:00, 8:00, 9:00, 10:00, 12:00; weekdays, 6:00, 8:00; Saturdays 9:00. Visitors welcome. Time: allow 15 minutes. For visits during the afternoon, inquire at the rectory, 218 Queen Street, next door to the church.

Continue north on South Hancock Street and turn west on the north side of Queen Street. Cross Second Street. Between Second and Third on the south side is the sandstone **St. Philip Neri Church (5)**.

Built in 1840 in Greek Revival style, this handsome church was designed by Eugene Napoleon Le Brun (1821–1901). Of French parentage and something of a prodigy, Le Brun was placed in the office of Thomas Ustick Walter to learn his profession. By the time he was twenty-one he was in business for himself. But he designed St. Philip Neri Church at the age of nineteen, before leaving Walter's employ.

Le Brun's design has a hint of the baroque, which he was to carry out further in his ambitious Cathedral of SS. Peter and Paul at Logan Circle. It is a design devised with great finesse. Four pilasters support an entablature and pediment in the usual way, but the spaces between are broken up with restrained imagination. Stained glass windows gaze at us like jeweled eyes. The finely wrought iron hinges and handles of unusual design on the three great doors were probably added much later. Another unusual touch is the gold "IHS A.D. 1840" above the main entrance and the splendidly triumphant cross rising above the pediment.

The interior is grand in manner and has a fine fresco of the Resurrection and an altarpiece depicting the Creation by the Italian painter Nicola Monachesi (1795–1851). Monachesi, who came to Philadelphia in 1831 and liked it enough to stay, executed his first commission for William Strickland—a fresco for the ceiling of the Exchange Room of the Philadelphia Exchange. He also painted frescoes and altarpieces for other Roman Catholic churches, including St. Mary's, St. Joseph's, and St. Augustine's.

Shortly after the church was completed, it became one of the main targets for the anti-Irish mobs in the Philadelphia Riots of 1844. Irish immigration had increased dramatically, jumping from 54,238 for 1821–1830 to a record 207,381 for 1831–1840. Settling largely in coastal cities like Philadelphia, New York, and Boston, the Catholic Irish provided the cheap labor necessary for the rapid growth of these cities. Traditional religious tolerance broke down as native Americans lost their jobs. To make matters worse, an anti-Catholic party fanned the resentment. Members of the Native American party, a forerunner of the Know-Nothing Movement, organized riots, in Philadelphia as elsewhere, to demand that immigration be subject to control and that naturalized citizens be barred from holding office. St. Augustine's Roman Catholic Church, in the north of the city, was burned. A street battle broke out along Queen Street, but order was restored before St. Philip Neri could meet with a similar end.

Walk through the pleasantly shaded Mario Lanza Park. Turn right on Catherine Street and continue east to Second.

Neziner Synagogue

771 South Second Street between Fitzwater and Catherine streets. Open to the public. Inquiries should be made of the sexton at No. 769.

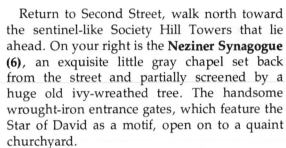

Return to Second Street, walk north toward the sentinel-like Society Hill Towers that lie ahead. On your right is the **Neziner Synagogue (6)**, an exquisite little gray chapel set back from the street and partially screened by a huge old ivy-wreathed tree. The handsome wrought-iron entrance gates, which feature the Star of David as a motif, open on to a quaint churchyard.

The church, whose architect is unknown, was erected in 1809–1810 by the Third Baptist Church and was the first all-stone building in Southwark. It served as the Southwark Baptist Church from 1810 to 1898, was occupied by the Polish National Society for a time, then was purchased and restored by the Congregation Ahavas Achim Nazin Misach Hoarce, a group of Jews from Nezine, Poland, in 1905.

The interior, with freshly painted walls and much original woodwork, contains symmetrically aligned pews. A fine staircase leads to a seating gallery on three sides, and a great chandelier hangs from an elaborate ceiling rose.

We have now completed our tour of Southwark. Continuing north along Second Street, we return to our starting point—Head House Square.

Walk 5

Round and About Washington Square

DISTANCE: 2 miles. TIME: 1 to 2 hours, again depending on how many buildings you enter.

This tour begins and ends in Washington Square, one of the five in Penn's original city plan. It is, perhaps, the most beautiful of all, with its shady trees, inquisitive squirrels, and Federal-era houses at the southwest end. It is reminiscent of the Washington Square of the 1840s, which was the center of the most affluent and fashionable neighborhood of Philadelphia. Much has been torn down. On the south side, for example, Hopkinson House, a tall, modern apartment house, replaced Washington Square Church, designed by John Haviland and one of the finest Greek Revival churches in the city. One can only take comfort that "so priceless a treasure," as one historian described the church, would not be razed today.

Next door to Hopkinson House, America's oldest publishing house, Lea and Febiger (★), still stands. The firm was founded in 1785 as Carey, Lea and Blanchard, the publishers of many famous authors, including Dickens, Poe, Washington Irving, and Thackeray.

On the east side, another celebrated publishing house, J. B. Lippincott, faces the square at No. 227. No. 225, next door, is a reconstruction of a Colonial house, the former residence of Mayor Richardson Dilworth (★). And along-

side is the handsome brownstone Athenaeum of Philadelphia.

As you turn to walk west on Walnut Street, you will pass the massive white marble Curtis Publishing Company building (★), a reminder of the days, fairly recent, when Philadelphia was an important center of magazine publishing. Here was the home of the *Saturday Evening Post*, *Ladies' Home Journal*, *Country Gentleman*, and *Holiday*. Do not miss taking a look at the Maxfield Parrish glass mosaic mural in the lobby. Entitled *The Dream Garden*, it is fifteen feet high and almost fifty feet long, and was executed by the Louis C. Tiffany Studios in 1916. Maxfield Parrish (1870–1966), one of the most original American painter-illustrators of the early twentieth century, was a Philadelphian. His ancestors date back to the days of William Penn. Across the street, on the corner of Washington Square and Walnut is the Philadelphia Savings Fund Society building, erected in 1869, whose first home we saw on Walk 1.

Before you leave the square at Locust Street, look across at the row of houses on the north side of Walnut between Seventh and Eighth streets (★). These are the work of the celebrated architect Benjamin Latrobe (1764–1820), known as the American Christopher Wren.

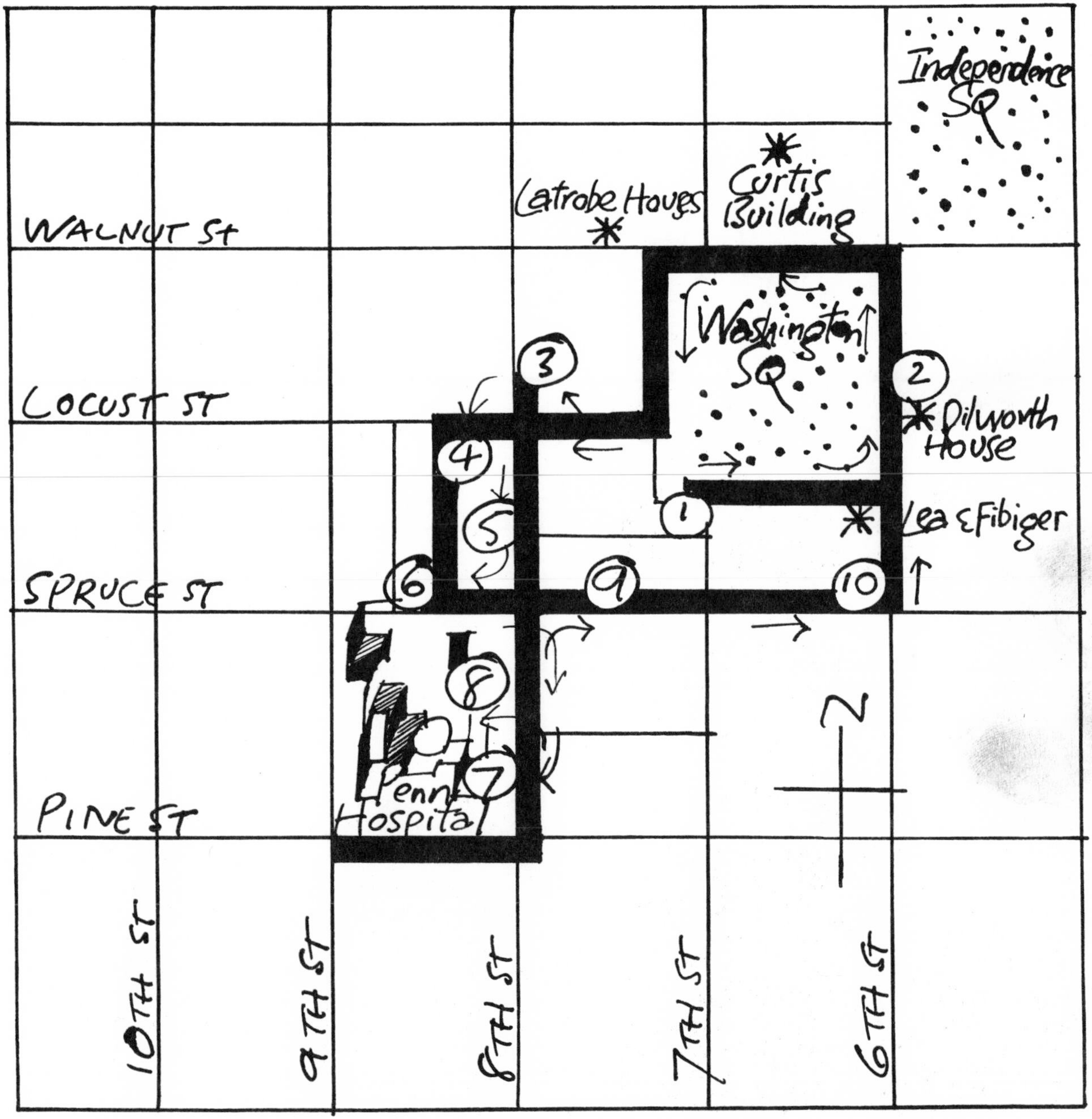

Independence SQ
Curtis Building
Latrobe Houses
WALNUT ST
Washington SQ
LOCUST ST
Dilworth House
Lea & Fibiger
SPRUCE ST
Penn Hospital
PINE ST
N
10TH ST
9TH ST
8TH ST
7TH ST
6TH ST
1
2
3
4
5
6
7
8
9
10

South Washington Square

In William Penn's Philadelphia, Quakers didn't name squares after people. Washington Square in 1825 and gradually began to acquire until 1825. Nor was it always as elegant as it later became. From 1705 until after the Revolution, the square was a vast burial ground, the resting place of the two thousand American and British soldiers as well as many victims of the yellow fever epidemic of 1793. The northeast corner was the site of the Walnut Street Prison. The square was renamed Washington Square in 1825 and gradually began to acquire a more residential character.

The quiet, shaded southwest corner gives an idea of what Federal Philadelphia must have been like. One building stands out: the **Meredith-Penrose House (1)**. This handsome mansion on the southwest corner of South Washington Square and Seventh Street dates back to 1823. Its builder and first owner was the Philadelphia merchant Asaph Stone, obviously a man of taste and with the means to exercise it. The splendid, dignified interior contains many examples of superb craftsmanship: ornate plaster ceilings, mahogany doors, and many magnificent fireplaces. Note also the cast-iron railings above the basement and the cast-iron trellis that embellishes the rear porch. (Not open to the public.)

Farther along, in the third house from the corner of Seventh Street (just where a man is walking his dog in my picture), the famous novelist and journalist Christopher Morley (1890–1957) lived when young and not yet famous.

The Athenaeum

219 South Sixth Street. For free guided group tour call WA 5-2688. Open Monday through Friday 9:00–4:00. Closed Saturdays, Sundays, and holidays. Time: 30 minutes.

Named for the more peaceful functions of the Greek Goddess, the **Philadelphia Athenaeum (2)** is one of the few remaining examples in the United States of a unique Victorian institution: an association of persons of literary, scientific, and artistic attainments—patrons of learning—established in the context of an elegant and comfortable clubhouse.

It was designed by John Notman (1810–1865), following a keenly contested competition in which Strickland, Haviland, Walter, and Le Brun took part. Notman was thirty-five years old at the time and had considerably less of a reputation, but his was the only design in the new Italian Renaissance Revival style favored by Sir Charles Barry (1795 – 1860) for his London Travellers Club (1829), Manchester Athenaeum (1836), London Reform Club (1837), and the Boston Athenaeum, which was being built at the same time.

Notman was born in Edinburgh and served his architectural apprenticeship there at the Royal Institution and later at Michael Angelo Nicholson's School of Architecture and Perspective in London. He emigrated to Philadelphia in 1831, while his brother went to Montreal and established himself there as a successful photographer. Originally designed for marble but changed to brownstone to reduce the cost, Notman's Athenaeum was the first of its kind in Philadelphia. It is balanced and dignified, with majestic steps set in molded checkblocks topped by stone balls that lead to an entrance hall graced with a superb Empire pier table and an elegant mirror. A magnificent wood stairway with banisters of cast iron ascends to spacious reading rooms with splendid views overlooking a secluded garden at the rear and the shaded serenity of Washington Square at the front.

Wherever you look, treasures meet the eye. Since 1847 the Athenaeum has been enriched with important collections of paintings, statuary, and period furniture. There are portraits by John Neagle (1796–1865), and fine chairs that originally graced Joseph Bonaparte's Philadelphia home. Note the massive octagonal chess tables in the Library Room, thought to have been designed by Notman himself. They proved to be a bone of contention in the early days, and members were warned that chess playing was not to interfere with the use of the room by the directors for their business meetings. Surrounded by such carpeted splendor, it is hard to imagine that only nine days after opening, the directors felt obliged to remind members of the need to preserve silence in the rooms and not to place their feet on the tables or chairs.

The Reynolds-Morris House

225 South Eighth Street between Walnut and Spruce streets. Not open to the public.

Proceed north around Washington Square to the west side, leaving the square at Locust Street. Continue west on Locust Street, turn right at Eighth Street, and walk a few steps to pause and view the **Reynolds-Morris House (3)**, built by John Reynolds, 1786–1787, and later bought by Luke Wistar Morris, son of Captain Samuel Morris of Germantown. This elegant old house passed through several generations of the Morris family until World War II, at which time it was bought by N. W. Ayer & Son, Inc., the well-known Philadelphia advertising agency, and used as a guesthouse for important visitors. It is now a private residence again, the home of Dr. Frank Elliott, the world-famous neurosurgeon, and his wife. Seeing me drawing the house, they were kind enough to show me around, a gesture that enabled me to note that the interior had kept its original character.

Characteristically, the house is built of Flemish bond brick with alternating black headers and red stretchers. A great molded box cornice with rainwater heads, dated 1787, enhances the frontage as does the beautiful doorway with its fluted pilasters and exquisite fanlight. Two windows flank the doorway, with four on the second and third floors plus three shed dormers in the gable roof above.

The unexpected bonus of the original garden, full of old trees and shrubs and enclosed by handsomely styled wrought-iron railings, sets off what is a perfectly preserved example of a patrician town house, pre-Revolutionary in character and Colonial in style.

Musical Fund Hall

806 Locust Street. Not open to the public.

Leaving the Reynolds-Morris House behind, return to Locust Street. To the west, on the south side of Locust, is the **Musical Fund Hall (4)**, once the city's main concert hall and now standing pathetically debased and unoccupied amid a wasteland of several recently demolished blocks. Even though experts have urged a variety of uses for this famous building, its future was still very much in doubt at the time I made my picture.

Originally an uncompleted church, and remodeled by several architects—Strickland in 1824, Le Brun in 1847, and Addison Hutton in 1891—Musical Fund Hall was the scene of many historical events, both political and cultural. Until 1857, when the Academy of Music opened for business, the hall's annual concerts attracted the cream of Philadelphia society. The building itself grew out of the Musical Fund Society, founded in 1820 by a circle of music lovers who had the habit of performing in each other's homes. The circle included the painter Thomas Sully and Francis Drexel, also a painter as well as the founder of the celebrated Drexel Company. From these private concerts came the idea of sponsoring public concerts to present the best that Europe and America had to offer. Duly incorporated February 23, 1823, the society's objectives were announced as "the cultivation of skill and diffusion of taste in music and the relief of [needy] musicians and their families."

From the time of its opening in 1824 to the beginning of the Civil War in 1861, more artists and celebrities of every kind appeared on its stage than in any other hall or theatre in America. The singers included soprano Jenny Lind, the legendary "Swedish Nightingale," launched in America by P. T. Barnum. Various conventions and lectures brought prominent statesmen and celebrated men of letters. The first Republican Party National Convention met here in 1856 and nominated 43-year-old John Charles Frémont for president. A host of writers lectured on a wide variety of topics. The lecturers included Ralph Waldo Emerson, Charles Dickens, William Makepeace Thackeray, and Arthur Conan Doyle, creator of the immortal Sherlock Holmes.

Musical Fund Hall was sold some time during the 1950s. Efforts to make it a National Museum of Music failed, so it became the warehouse and office of a cigar manufacturer. Even though the facade has been altered slightly and its fine old gas lamps removed, you can still imagine early Philadelphians gathering of an evening to hear Jenny Lind or Charles Dickens.

Greek Orthodox Cathedral of St. George

250 South Eighth Street between Locust and Spruce streets. Open daily 9:00–5:00. Free guided tours. Call at office, 250 South Eighth Street, or telephone WA 2-9122. Time: allow 25 minutes.

Return to Eighth Street and walk south. On the west side of the street you will see the white columns of Philadelphia's most graceful Greek Revival building. Designed by Haviland and built in 1822 for the use of St. Andrew's Protestant Episcopal congregation, it now serves the city's large Greek community and has been renamed the **Greek Orthodox Cathedral of St. George (5)**.

John Haviland, whose work we have already encountered, designed many other superb buildings in Philadelphia, but his finest and his own favorite was St. Andrew's. It was Haviland's own congregation and he is buried beneath the church. His grave was discovered by the Reverend Demetrios Katerlis, who, carried away by the rehabilitation of Old Philadel-

phia, decided to initiate his own research program. His excavation of the huge crypt in 1960 revealed the last resting place of the architect.

Haviland based his design on the Temple of Bacchus at Teos, Greece. Six splendid Ionic columns support the entablature, which is enriched by bands of sculptured decoration. The huge pediment is edged by an acanthus frieze and topped by a large gold cross. If this is not impressive enough, there is a great entrance door, and a superbly designed cast-iron fence. The interior, with galleries on three sides, is supported by cast-iron columns reached by handsome stairways from the vestibule. The rectory, or office, on the left-hand side of the church, was added in 1840.

112

Mikveh Israel Cemetery

Northwest corner of Spruce and Darien streets. Open to the public by appointment only. Telephone: DA 4-9350. Time: 15 minutes.

Turn right at Spruce and walk on the north side. Opposite the modern annex of the Pennsylvania Hospital is the brick-walled **Mikveh Israel Cemetery (6)**, built in 1740. This peaceful oasis was the old burial ground of the Spanish-Portuguese Jewish community and the oldest surviving Jewish historic site in colonial Philadelphia. Although the cemetery is part of the Independence National Historic Park, you have to be content with peeping through the closed iron gates and reading the historic marker erected by the Pennsylvania Historical Commission.

The marker states that notables buried here include Nathan Levy, whose ship brought the Liberty Bell to America; Haym Solomon, Revolutionary patriot; the Gratz family; and Aaron Levy, founder of Aaronsburg. But there are many more: twenty-one soldiers of the Revolutionary War, among them Philip Moses Russel, surgeon's mate at Valley Forge during the memorable bitter winter of 1777–1778; Benjamin Nones, who served as a staff officer under Washington and Lafayette and was later a major of the Hebrew Legion; and Cushman Pollock, who also fought in the Revolutionary War.

But of all the illustrious people of the Congregation Mikveh Israel who lie here, the one whose life was the most inspiring was the devoted patriot, Haym Solomon (1740–1785), whose unstinted financial support, through Robert Morris, of the Revolutionary cause, has only recently been fully recognized. Even before he arrived in Philadelphia, while living in British-occupied New York, he helped French and American prisoners escape to the American lines. The story is told of the time Robert Morris, then financing the struggle for independence, was in dire need of money. It was Yom Kippur, the holiest day for the Jews worshipping in Mikveh Israel. The Orthodox Jews gathered there were naturally forbidden even to think of money. Yet, when Morris went to Solomon and told him that thousands of dollars were in danger of being discounted, Solomon mounted the rostrum to make an appeal for support, to which the congregation responded without reservation.

Certainly the most romantic person who lies here is Rebecca Gratz (1781–1869). It was she who was the inspiration of Sir Walter Scott's heroine Rebecca, in his classic novel *Ivanhoe*. He had learned of her from Washington Irving, who described her as a young and singularly beautiful Jewish woman who had loved and been loved by a Christian but who would not marry out of her faith and had, therefore, devoted her life and her great wealth to helping others.

Perhaps the most tragic persons who lie here in unmarked graves are those "poor dead soldiers of King George," to use Kipling's words, who were lined up against the wall and shot for desertion and other offenses.

Pennsylvania Hospital

Between Spruce and Pine, Eighth and Ninth streets (entrance on Eighth). Open to the public Monday and Wednesday 9:00–4:00 by appointment only. Telephone 829-3251 for free guided tour. Time: allow at least 30 minutes.

Walking back to the intersection of Eighth and Spruce streets, you will pass some of the more modern buildings of the Pennsylvania Hospital, but the original Colonial buildings stand within a whole walled city block a little farther south. Walk down Eighth Street to Pine to get the best overall view of one of the finest examples of eighteenth-century public buildings in America, surpassing Independence Hall itself in its elegant majesty.

Pennsylvania Hospital (7) was founded in 1751 by a circle of public-spirited citizens led by Benjamin Franklin and Dr. Thomas Bond. It was built between 1755 and 1805, and is the oldest hospital in the United States. The original buildings, some still in use, housed the first medical library, operating amphitheatre, and public dispensary. Our old friend Samuel Rhoads designed the original hospital building, now the east wing, as well as the imposing Pine Street facade of the administration building with its huge octagonal drum and balustrade top and its stately wings, each with lantern towers and flamboyant weathervanes. The central building, approached through the main gateway on Eighth Street, is thought to have been the work of John Dorsey, a wealthy auctioneer and amateur architect.

On the lawn, in front of the tree-shaded facade facing Pine, is a quaint lead statue of William Penn. Whoever created this endearing figure is a mystery. It was first discovered by

William Penn. Sculptor unknown.

Franklin in 1775 during his final stay in England as agent for Massachusetts and Pennsylvania. As deputy postmaster general for North America, he had become friendly with Lord Le Despencer, the postmaster general of England, spending welcome weekends at his country house at West Wycombe near London, where the statue graced the palatial grounds. Le Despencer offered the statue to Franklin for fifty pounds, but nothing further is known about it until 1804 when John Penn, grandson of William, bought it in a London junk shop and presented it to the hospital.

As in the case of the Franklin statue that stood in front of the original Library Hall on Fifth Street and was said to step down from its niche at midnight to enjoy a tankard of beer on a neighboring fire hydrant, so it is said that Old Bill Penn steps down to take a turn about the hospital grounds on New Year's Eve after the clock strikes midnight.

There are many objects of interest to see in the hospital. For example, Benjamin West's famous *Christ Healing the Sick*, painted in 1817, which raised $25,000 for the hospital when put on exhibition; the celebrated Fothergill Collection of seventeen anatomical crayon drawings by the famous Dutch painter Van Riemsdyk, a vivid reminder of the vital role played by eighteenth-century artists in the training of surgeons and doctors.

Be sure to glance at the legendary **Treaty Elm (8)**, a direct descendant of the Great Elm of Kensington, under which William Penn made his perpetual treaty of friendship with the Indians. The original elm was destroyed by a storm but a part of its root was given to the hospital and a new elm came up. This second elm had to be cut down, but cuttings were taken and the present tree grew from one of those cuttings.

The Treaty Elm

Whitten Evans House

715 Spruce Street between Seventh and Eighth. Not open to the public.

Return to Spruce and walk east toward Seventh. On the north side of the street is the **Whitten Evans House (9)**, a handsome building of the Federal period. Built in 1821 by Whitten Evans, a wealthy merchant, the house first belonged to Evans and then, about 1830, became the town house of Nicholas Biddle during his term as president of the Second Bank of the United States.

Biddle lived here during the period he was actively involved in his celebrated confrontation with Andrew Jackson. Under his efficient direction, the bank had become a rich and immensely powerful institution, enjoying a monopoly of government deposits totaling $40 million a year, with profits as high as $1.5 million—huge amounts for those days. The bank's charter came up for renewal in 1836 and, though granted by Congress, Jackson vetoed it in his famous the-poor-against-the-rich message. The second bank soon became a memory. A new bank was organized, and the United States Bank of Pennsylvania opened for business with Biddle as president. But when this also failed, he resigned and retired to his country estate at Andalusia, near Bristol in Bucks County. The house, however, remained, in the Biddle family for long afterward.

Biddle's greatest love was architecture, and his passion for the classical was a source of great encouragement to those architects—notably Strickland, Haviland, and Walter—who practiced the Greek Revival style. To Biddle must be given much of the credit for the development of a national architecture and for Philadelphia's leading role in the movement.

Holy Trinity Church

At the northwest corner of Spruce and Sixth streets is **Holy Trinity Roman Catholic Church (10)**, which was opened for services in 1789 by a German congregation. The first Catholic orphan asylum was opened here in 1789 by the church, and "the little Catholic churchyard in the heart of the city" referred to in Longfellow's poem *Evangeline* is this one.

Walk 6

Between Washington Square and Broad Street

DISTANCE: about 2 miles. TIME: 2 hours or more, depending on the length of your visit to the museum of the Historical Society of Pennsylvania and your interest in strolling down old shaded, cobblestoned back streets, not to mention browsing in antique shops.

Again Washington Square is the starting point for this last tour—an excursion through a most fascinating district of Old Philadelphia: the section bounded by Sixth and Fourteenth streets, and Walnut and Pine. Here is a picturesque maze of tiny back streets and of old houses newly restored, which were fearsome slums not so long ago. Many cul-de-sacs, with ivy growing round windows, doors, and fences, are inhabited largely by young families or students from the nearby College of Art on Broad and Pine streets. Automobiles cannot pass without difficulty as a single vehicle can fill the road from curb to curb.

This tour also includes a visit to the oldest playhouse in America, the Walnut Street Theatre, and to the numerous clubs that have earned Philadelphia the title the "City of Clubs." There are more social organizations of that character here than in any other city in the United States—indeed, in the world, except for London. The bigger clubs are mostly to the west of Broad, outside the Old City. But we will be seeing many others on our walk, particularly on Camac Street, which is known as "the Street of Little Clubs."

We begin at the northwest corner of Washington Square, walking west on Walnut Street to Ninth and our first stop, the Walnut Street Theatre.

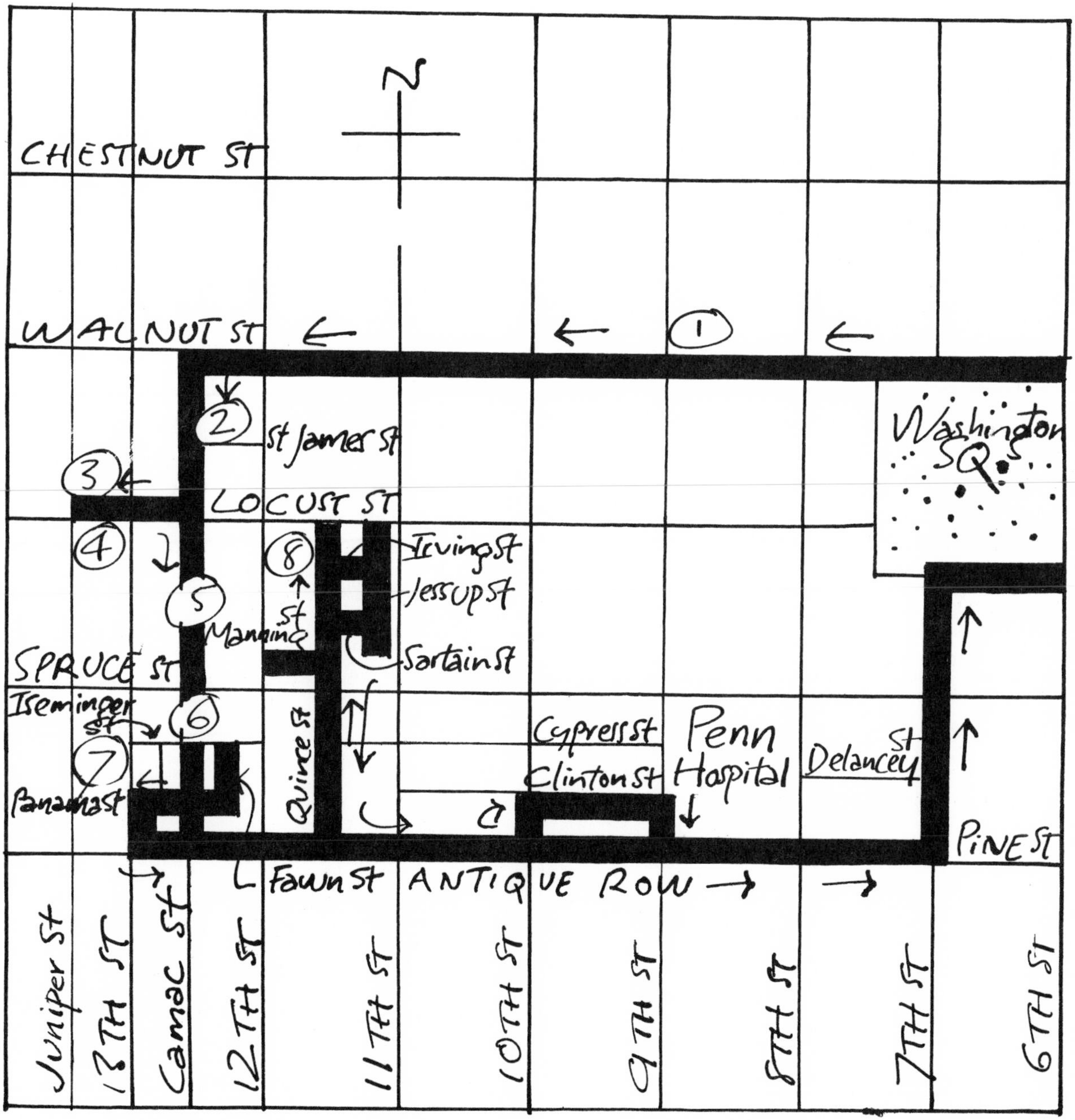
N
CHESTNUT ST
WALNUT ST
1
2
St James St
3
LOCUST ST
4
5
8
Irving St
Jessup St
Manning St
Sartain St
SPRUCE ST
Iseminger St
6
7
Panama St
Quince St
Cypress St
Clinton St
Penn Hospital
Delancey St
Washington SQ
PINE ST
Fawn St
ANTIQUE ROW
Juniper St
13TH ST
Camac St
12TH ST
11TH ST
10TH ST
9TH ST
8TH ST
7TH ST
6TH ST

Walnut Street Theatre

Northeast corner of Ninth and Walnut streets. Telephone: WA 5-6855.

An all-year-round, performing arts center for music, drama, ballet, and movies. Participating city and state groups include the Pennsylvania Ballet Company; and the American Dance Festival brings famous ballet companies from time to time. See local newspapers for current programs. There are movies every Saturday morning throughout the year at 11:00, with full-length feature films specially selected for the young in heart.

The historic **Walnut Street Theatre (1)** was designed by John Haviland and opened in 1808 as the New Circus. A stage was added in 1811, and the first play performed in 1812. When the rival Chestnut Street Theatre burned down in 1820, the building, now known as the Olympic, was renamed the Walnut Street Theatre. After the Theatre Royal in Drury Lane, London, built 1809–1812 by Benjamin Wyatt, it is the oldest playhouse in the English-speaking world. Like that only surviving theatre of Georgian London, the Walnut has a great past. Edwin Forrest made his debut and final appearance here. Edmund Kean, Otis Skinner, Edwin Booth, George Arliss, Lily Langtry, and John and Ethel Barrymore all appeared on the stage of the Walnut. Sarah Bernhardt caught a cold in one of its original drafty dressing rooms. Seriously ill, she returned to France to die.

The interior was remodeled in 1920 and again in 1972. The firm of Rohm and Hass, Philadelphia manufacturers of plexiglass and acrylics, restored the facade to something like the Haviland original.

Franklin Inn Club

205 South Camac Street. Not open to the public; you must be invited by a member.

Continue west on Walnut. Just past Twelfth Street turn south on Camac. On the northeast corner of Camac and St. James streets is the **Franklin Inn Club (2)**, a men's club founded in 1902 by the well-known historical novelist S. Weir Mitchell (1829–1914), and his friends. Among the famous Philadelphia writers who were members were Christopher Morley, Joseph Hergesheimer, and Poultney Bigelow. Its vigorous fellowship has now been extended to artists, newspapermen, and academics, indeed to all contributing to the literary, artistic, and intellectual life of the city.

The exterior resembles an English north-country inn. The house was originally two properties erected in 1795 as houses for Richard Wistar, merchant and member of the board of directors of the Library Company of Philadelphia, and Francis Higgins, a weaver. It was bought by the Franklin Inn Club in 1907.

The interior has kept much of its original character, enhanced with the club's rich collections of memorabilia, including caricatures of famous Philadelphia writers and editors. I lunched here one day in convivial company, and I wish I had been hard-nosed enough to depict its long low dining room, wood paneled and with great beams across the ceiling. Perhaps one day I shall.

Clarence Bloomfield Moore House

1321 Locust Street. Northeast corner of Locust and Juniper streets. Now a restaurant.

Continue on Camac Street to Locust. Go west on Locust and walk past Thirteenth Street to Juniper to view the **Clarence Bloomfield House (3)**, a magnificent feat of architectural fantasy. The architect was Wilson Eyre (1858–1940), famous for the whimsical quality of his buildings, largely built in 1890s Philadelphia.

Eyre was typically Victorian in that he borrowed from every country and from every period, and blended them together with extraordinary skill. The corner tower with its conical roof, the huge dominating chimney stacks, the medallions and gargoyles, the deep-set arched windows of thick colored glass, the immensely complex brickwork resting on a banded rusticated limestone base, all add up to a masterpiece of Victorian romantic eclecticism.

The house was built in the early 1890s for Clarence Bloomfield Moore, wealthy merchant, world traveler, amateur anthropologist, and man-about-town noted for his sumptuous hospitality. Here Moore assembled a vast collection of furniture and objects, trophies and memorabilia, now unfortunately scattered to the winds. Such houses belong to the period in which they were conceived. To remove their furnishings and fixtures, even their vulgarities, to the safety of museums emasculates their peculiar charm. Much of the interior was also changed due to the occupancy of Bennie the Bum's Steak House. But at least we can be thankful that much remains. The Gothic-style central hall, stairway, and tiled floors are intact, as are numerous rooms.

Historical Society of Pennsylvania

Benjamin Franklin, after Giuseppe Ceracchi.

1300 Locust Street. Open to the public Monday 1:00–5:00; Tuesday through Friday 9:00–5:00; closed Saturdays, Sundays, holidays, and normally during the month of August. Admission $1.00. For major exhibits during the bicentenary year, ask at the Visitors Information Center or call 732-6200. Library open to the public. Time: allow one hour.

Occupying half a block on the south side of Locust at Thirteenth Street is the great rambling building of the **Historical Society of Pennsylvania (4).** Founded in 1824, the society maintains a treasure house of colonial and Revolutionary history. It is also an important research center for scholars undertaking studies of colonial family life. Its huge archives include early American histories, diaries, and business records, plus such endearingly personal manuscripts as Martha Washington's cookbook, with the recipes written in her own hand.

The museum is on the first floor and has several impressive collections that, by the time you make your visit, will have been reorganized as a special bicentenary exhibit with additional material from other American museums as well as from England and France.

Here antique buffs will be fascinated by the wide variety of fine furniture and objects unique in their intimate association with the American past, such as William Penn's chairs, desk, chest, the family cradle—even his razor—and, of course, the celebrated wampum belt given by the Indians of Pennsylvania as a token of friendship; Benjamin Franklin's silver tankard, made by Gurney and Cooke of London, 1754; Thomas Jefferson's grandfather clock, still ticking off the minutes; and the furniture George Washington used during the years he was president and lived in Philadelphia.

There is much more, including the first and second drafts of the Constitution. Note that the first draft, the work of the Philadelphia lawyer James Wilson does not include the familiar preamble: "We the people . . ."

The collection of paintings is in itself almost a survey of the colonial period. Along with works by lesser craftsmen are superlative works by several masters. Particularly notable is the fine double portrait of Thomas Mifflin and his wife Sarah Morris by John Singleton Copley (1738–1815); and a portrait of the tragic Margaret Shippen, who married Benedict Arnold, by the English master, Daniel Gardner.

George Washington, after William Rush by Beck.

133

The Street of Little Clubs

Camac Street between Locust and Spruce. The Charlotte Cushman Club is open to the public except June through August. Free guided tours are given Monday through Friday 2:00–5:00. The Plastic Club is open only when an exhibit is hung.

Walk east on Locust to Camac Street and turn right. You are now back in the **Street of Little Clubs (5),** part of which we visited earlier to look at the Franklin Inn Club. We walk down the narrow, old-fashioned alley, passing quaint red-brick, panel-shuttered houses on one side, some with signs like colonial taverns.

The first, No. 235, is the Sketch Club, the oldest professional artists' club in America, founded in 1860 by rebel students of the Academy of Fine Arts to promote "the freedom to sketch." Inside, the walls are covered with portraits of Philadelphia's artists over the last century. Howard Chandler Christy, N. C. Wyeth, and Joseph Pennell were members, as was the great Thomas Eakins.

At No. 239 is the Charlotte Cushman Club, a private club for actresses and named for the great nineteenth-century American actress, whose voice was said to possess "an unearthly music that made the nerves thrill and the brain tremble." The club has a nostalgic collection of paintings and memorabilia of actresses of the past, when Philadelphia was the theatrical capital of the nation.

Finally, at No. 247, is the Plastic Club, for women painters and sculptors. Founded in 1895, it is the oldest women's art club in America.

South Camac Street

Cross Spruce and continue south on Camac Street. **South Camac Street (6),** from here to Pine, is one of the most delightful streets in Old Philadelphia, with little houses of Colonial and Federal vintage on both sides, "an oasis of charm and gentility," to quote Nathaniel Burt. The original street, farther north, was laid out as Dean Street about 1756 and was named during the last century for the Camac family, long notable in the city. Captain Turner Camac (1751–1830) of County Down, Ireland, married Sarah Masters, the sister of Mrs. Richard Penn, in London in 1795, and he came here to supervise his wife's estate in 1804. A grandson, Dr. William Camac (1829–1900), was a founder of the Philadelphia Zoo in 1899. When street names were made uniform at the turn of the century, Camac was the name given this and all other small units on the same line. Note the different types of early firemarks, usually at the second-story level. If you have time, take a look at Iseminger and Fawn streets, tiny picturesque alleys to the right and left of South Camac.

Church of St. Luke and the Epiphany

330 South Thirteenth Street between Spruce and Pine. Open Monday through Friday 9:00–4:00. Time: 15 minutes.

Keep walking south on Camac, cross Cypress Street, then turn right and continue west on Panama. At the end of the street as you enter Thirteenth is the noble facade of the **Church of St. Luke and the Epiphany (7).** St. Luke and the Epiphany is a union of two Episcopal churches that were well known throughout the nineteenth century; the congregations merged in 1898. The churches had much in common and burned brightly with the practical zeal of evangelicalism. Rectors have included Dr. Stephen Higginson Tyng, a famous abolitionist, and Dr. William Robert Hare, who won national acclaim for his efforts on behalf of the Sioux Indians. The tradition continues to this day.

An example of Greek Revival in its last phase, the church was built between 1839 and 1840 on a square plan by Thomas S. Stewart, after a competition in which Strickland and Notman also entered plans. It is a design with unusual features: cast-iron Corinthian columns, narrow mullioned windows, and huge entrance doors, set off by a flight of steps and flanked by rusticated checkblocks graced by elegant lamps. The wall is embellished by a fine cast-iron fence. After visiting St. Luke's, walk south to Pine Street.

Quince Street
and Antique Row

Quince Street from Spruce.

140

Go east on Pine and turn left on **Quince Street (8)**, a picturesque cobbled alley linking Pine and Spruce. Here we dip into a vanished America, just five minutes away from busy Broad Street yet as tranquil as a small town. Stroll up Quince Street, which is lined with small houses from the Federal period and later, into Manning and Sartain streets. Then continue past tiny Irving Street and on to Jessup Street, a pretty cul-de-sac.

Go back to Pine again and walk east a block. Turn left at Eleventh Street to view Clinton Street with its superb houses from the Federal era. Then return to Eleventh Street and continue east along Pine. Between Eleventh and Ninth streets is Antique Row East, one of the city's two main districts. (Antique Row West lies on the other side of Broad Street.) Philadelphia is a big antique furniture center where prices are lower than elsewhere. Here you will find many shops, both wholesale and retail, dealing in a bewildering assortment of American and English antiques and good reproductions: pictures and bric-a-brac, old coins, dolls, uniforms, armor, and colonial warming pans. Most of these are specialty shops, but at Reese's, No. 928, the oldest in the street, almost anything can be found. Gargoyle's, 512 Third Street at Lombard (next block south of St. Peter's on Pine Street), has a large selection of old inn signs and colonial memorabilia. As far as I could make out, there is no agreed opening or closing time. Some open early, at 8:30; most by 10:00; and closing is between 5:00 and 5:30. Most are open all day Saturday during the summer.

On your way back to Washington Square you will pass Pennsylvania Hospital again. Be sure to look at the Victorian brownstones opposite, with their fine cast-iron railings and handrails.

Cross at Seventh Street and walk north. This will bring you back to your starting point.

Footscrapers

It would be a monumental task to catalog the many different types of footscrapers to be seen in the streets of Old Philadelphia. Instead, I have made a selection that I hope will inspire you to note the fine ironwork characteristic of Colonial and Federal architecture. You can then go on to make your own discoveries.

Philadelphia had streets much earlier than other cities in the Colonies, but some years passed before they were all paved and had sidewalks. Even in such a downtown district as Society Hill, shoes would get covered with mud crossing a busy street after a downfall of rain or snow. As rubber overshoes were then unknown it was necessary to remove the mud from your shoes before entering a house. Footscrapers on one side of the doorstep, or at the foot of the front steps, were the answer.

These were made of wrought iron well into the nineteenth century, but as the city grew, the demand far exceeded the capabilities of individual craftsmen. Later types were more elaborate and were cast in molds. Early wrought-iron types consisted of two upright standards with a sharp-edged horizontal bar between, the scraper itself. Sometimes a footscraper was part of the iron stair rail or newel post of the handrail.

One favorite design consisted of a large inverted U-shaped frame, with a spiral ornament applied in the Florentine manner. Another used two large spirals, in themselves the supports for the scraper bar.

The introduction of cast iron as a technique for mass production made it possible to produce more elaborate designs while keeping

footscrapers modest in size. Note the differences from house to house, and the types of houses: for example, the modest two-and-a-half-story town house, patrician houses like the Reynolds-Morris House, and such public buildings as banks.

Colonial footscrapers. (Above) Southwark. Wrought iron, circa 1750; (below) Barclay-Rhoads House, 217 Delancey Street. Wrought iron, circa 1760.

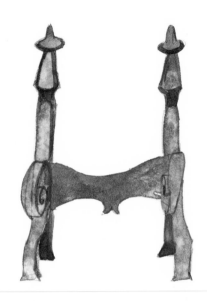

Colonial. Reynolds-Morris House, 225 South Eighth Street. Wrought iron, 1786.

Federal. First Bank of the United States, 116 South Third Street. Wrought iron, circa 1795–1797.

Federal. 236 South Third Street. Wrought iron, circa 1824.

Colonial style. 226 Spruce Street. Wrought iron, circa 1790–1800.

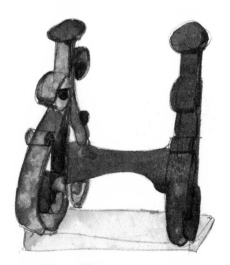

143

Federal. 229 Pine Street. Wrought iron, circa 1830.

Federal. First Pennsylvania Bank, 304 Walnut Street. Wrought iron, circa 1840.

Federal (Greek Revival) footscrapers. (Below left) 268 South Third Street. Cast iron, circa 1840; (right) 314 Philip Street. Cast iron, circa 1840.

144

Hitching Posts

In colonial America, hitching posts were vital necessities. At first, simple round or square wooden posts, with or without iron rings for reins, served the purpose. Wrought-iron types followed with plain or corkscrew newel posts. But the golden age of the hitching post began when cast iron came into its own. As private carriages increased rapidly in number, the demand became so great that there was no time for the slower traditional methods of craftsmanship. A simple model served to produce cast-iron reproductions in quantities.

From the basic newel post, more elaborate types were developed with a molded base and a plain or fluted shaft terminating in a ball or a horse's head. The hitching post had arrived and had become a symbol of status or success. More exotic types followed. Shafts were cast in the shape of swans or tree trunks, and finally figures of youthful jockeys, barefoot black or Oriental boys holding out the rings to which the reins were tied.

These more flamboyant types have vanished from the streets of Old Philadelphia and have recently become valuable relics much sought after by collectors. Some can still be seen in restaurants or gardens of private homes, but those to be seen on our walks (Society Hill is the richest section) are mainly cast-iron types dating from the Federal period to the Civil War.

See how many different types you can spot.

Colonial style. Barclay-Rhoads House, 217 Delancey Street. Wrought iron, modern reproduction.

Federal Commercial. South Camac Street. Cast iron, 1830–1840.

145

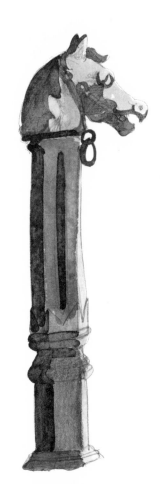

Federal swan neck. Hopkinson House, 338 Spruce Street. Cast iron, 1830–1840.

Victorian Horsehead. South Camac Street. Cast iron, 1850–1860

Victorian Horsehead. Delancey Street. Cast iron, 1860–1870.

146

Firemarks

American insurance firemarks date back to 1752. The idea was borrowed from England to identify insured buildings from those not insured.

The firemark was mounted on wood and nailed up in a prominent place, about level with the second-story windows. An insurance company's firemark was intended to discourage arson by showing that the owner himself would not suffer if the building was burned down. The firemark also stood as a guarantee to all fire brigades that the insurance company concerned would reward the volunteer brigade putting the fire out. When Philadelphia established the first paid municipal Fire Department in 1871, firemarks lost their function and were discontinued.

In themselves, the firemarks are delightful examples of Americana and have since become valuable heirlooms. Like stamps, there are many variants of a given definitive design, some being truly unique.

My illustrations are the five basic designs you are likely to notice during the walks. You will, of course, spot others. If this is the case, you may require more information and should visit the museum of the Insurance Company of North America at 1600 Arch Street. Here you will be given an excellent free informal tour of the best collection in Philadelphia. Open daily, Monday through Friday, 9:00–4:00. Call ahead, 251-4000 if you are in a group.

Buses: Loop, Cultural Loop, A local, No. 2 on Kennedy Boulevard/Market Street routes.

For two other museums with collections of firemarks, see Philadelphia Contributionship for the Insurance of Houses from Loss by Fire (page 59) and the Fire Department Museum (page 43).

Philadelphia Contributionship. Carpenters' Hall. Lead, circa 1765. Rare. Later variants of iron. This company, which is still in existence, issued a great number of variants. During the Revolution many were torn down by the British and the lead hands melted down for bullets.

Mutual Assurance Company. INA Collection. Iron with hollow back, circa 1810. Common. Earlier variants in lead. Mutual, founded in 1784, is also still going strong and owes its existence, its firemark, and its nickname— "The Green Tree" —to the fact that it would insure buildings surrounded by live trees, which the Contributionship would not.

Insurance Company of North America. INA Collection. Iron, circa 1830. Rare. Earlier variants in lead and copper. Founded in 1792 at Independence Hall, it was the first stock fire and marine insurance company in the country.

Fire Association of Philadelphia. INA Collection. Last issue of this company. Iron, circa 1870. Common. Earlier variants in lead and brass. This company, founded in 1817, was originally an association of volunteer fire companies that sought to make themselves self-supporting by the profits. It is still in existence.

United Firemen's Insurance Company. INA collection. Iron, circa 1860. Variants have different size fire engines. Rare. This company, which wound up its activities in 1953, was established in 1860 by members of the old volunteer fire companies. It issued firemarks for only ten years.

Lumbermen's Insurance Company. INA Collection. Iron, circa 1873. Common. The Lumbermen's Company was founded 1873, about the time that the days of the old volunteer fire companies were already numbered. This was the last company to use the firemark. The company is still doing business.

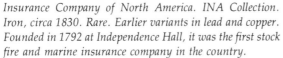

For Further Reading

BULAU, ALWIN E. *Footprints of Assurance.* New York: Home Insurance Company of New York, 1953.

BURT, NATHANIEL. *The Perennial Philadelphians.* Boston: Little, Brown, and Co., 1963.

BUTTERFIELD, ROGER, ed. *The American Past.* New York: Simon and Schuster, 1947.

COOKE, ALISTAIR. *Alistair Cooke's America.* New York: Alfred A. Knopf, 1973.

CROWE, EYRE. *With Thackeray in America.* London: 1893.

DICKENS, CHARLES. *American Notes.* Philadelphia: 1843 and subsequent editions.

EISENHART, LUTHER, ed. *Historic Philadelphia.* Transactions of the American Philosophical Society. Vol. 43, Part I. Philadelphia: 1953.

FLEMING, THOMAS. *The Man Who Dared the Lightning: A New Look at Benjamin Franklin.* New York: Wm. Morrow and Co., 1971.

FRANKLIN, BENJAMIN. *Some Account of the Pennsylvania Hospital 1751 – 1956.* Edited by I. Bernard Cohen. Baltimore: Johns Hopkins Press, 1957.

GILCHRIST, AGNES. *William Strickland: Architect and Engineer.* Philadelphia: University of Pennsylvania Press, 1950.

KIPLING, RUDYARD. *Rewards and Fairies* (New York: Doubleday, Page & Company, 1910) contains "Philadelphia" and other poems of America.

LOVE, NANCY. *Philadelphia Magazine's Guide to Philadelphia.* Philadelphia: 1973.

MCCORKER, M. J. *The Historical Collection of the Insurance Company of North America.* Philadelphia: 1967.

MARION, JOHN FRANCIS. *Bicentennial City.* Princeton: The Pyne Press, 1974.

TRAUTMAN, FREDERICK. *"Philadelphia Bowled Clean Over:* Public Readings by Charles Dickens." *Pennsylvania Magazine of History and Biography,* October 1974.

WAINWRIGHT, NICHOLAS. ed. *Sculpture of a City: Philadelphia's Treasures in Bronze and Stone.* New York: Walker and Co., 1974.

WALLACE, PHILIP B. *Colonial Ironwork in Old Philadelphia.* New York: Peter Smith, 1930.

WURMAN, RICHARD SAUL, and GALLERY, JOHN A. *Man-Made Philadelphia: A Guide to Its Physical & Cultural Environment.* Cambridge, Mass.: MIT Press, 1972.

Glossary of Architectural Terms

Acanthus. Ornament based on the leaf of a thistle. Used on composite and Corinthian capitals and sometimes on a frieze. Greek Revival.

Antefix. Upright ornamented motif placed above the eaves or gutter to decorate ends of a roof ridge. Greek Revival.

Baluster. Small, usually bottle-shaped column that supports a parapet. Georgian Colonial.

Baroque. Period roughly 1600–1700; the term is also applied to painting, sculpture, music, literature, and life-style of the period.

Basilica. In medieval architecture, a church with a nave higher than its aisles. In early Christian architecture, with apse at one end. Name and form, Roman.

Belfry. Part of a tower or turret in which bells are hung. Georgian Colonial.

Classicism. Style or tendency originally derived from ancient Greece or Rome.

Colonial. Style developed in eastern United States by European colonists using classical elements.

Colonnade. A columned walk without arches; a feature of neoclassical architecture. Greek Revival.

Column. Vertical supporting member; in classical architecture it consists of a base, shaft, and capital.

Composite Capital. Most elaborate of five orders, having many variations. Combines volutes, or spiral scrolls, of the Ionic with the foliate bell of the Corinthian.

Corinthian Capital. Bell-shaped capital ornamented with acanthus, olive, or laurel leaves, from which eight small, spiral scrolls emerge. Shaft usually fluted.

Cornice. Upper member of an entablature, also a molded projection of wood that tops or finishes part to which it is fixed, e.g., a wall, door, or window.

Crypt. Underground burial place in churches.

Cupola. A small domed roof, or small domed turret built on a roof. Georgian Colonial.

Doric Capital. Plainest and most massive of five orders. Squat in proportion; the relationship between thickness and height is usually 1:4. Greek Revival.

Dormer. Roof window. Georgian Colonial. See *Shed Dormer.*

Drum. Circular or polygonal wall on which a dome rests. Georgian Colonial.

Eclectic. Style that doesn't belong to any period of the past but borrows freely from various sources.

Egyptian Revival. Use of Egyptian forms and ornament as a result of archaeological discoveries around 1800.

Entablature. In classical architecture, the architectural superstructure that rests upon the capital of a column, consisting of the architrave, the frieze, and the cornice.

Facade. Face or front of a building, especially principal front.

Fanlight. A semicircular or fan-shaped window above a Georgian door.

Fluting. Vertical grooving on the shaft of a column.

Frieze. Decorative band, usually horizontal, along a wall or entablature. May be painted, carved, ornamented, or figured.

Gargoyle. Carved waterspout in the form of a grotesque human or animal head, usually projecting from top of a wall.

Header. A brick or stone laid in a wall with its end toward the face of the wall.

Ionic Order. Greek style originating in the Ionian Islands; characterized by voluted capitals and canalized column shafts.

Lantern. Very top of a dome. Usually cylindrical or polygonal, with windows, and crowned with a small dome. Georgian Colonial.

Mullion. Vertical shaft of stone, iron, or lead, dividing lights or panes in a window. Greek Revival.

Narthex. A vestibule stretching across the main entrance of a church.

Neoclassical. A style that dominated Europe, 1760 – 1790, and was the product of a new interest in antiquity that resulted from archaeological discoveries in Rome, in newly excavated Herculaneum, Pompeii, and other places. Unlike their predecessors, who accepted a textbook view of antiquity, architects of a practicing style generally made firsthand investigation of the monuments themselves. In England, the leading exponents were Robert Adam, James "Athenian" Stuart, and Sir William Chambers. In the United States: Benjamin Latrobe, Charles Bulfinch, and William Strickland.

Order. Essential components of a complete order are a column base, a shaft, and a capital; and an entablature with architrave, frieze, and cornice. Size and proportion vary. Three Greek orders are Doric, Ionic, and Corinthian. The Romans added two more: Tuscan and Composite. See also entries under these headings.

Palladian. Style named for Andrea Palladio (1508 – 1580). Introduced to England by Inigo Jones in 1615, and from England it later spread to America. Georgian Colonial.

Parapet. Low wall at the edge of a bridge, gallery, balcony, or above the cornice of a building. Georgian Colonial.

Pediment. A low-pitched triangular gable usually above an entablature. Also used as ornamental feature above doors and windows.

Pilaster. Rectangular column projecting slightly from a wall. Georgian Colonial and Greek Revival.

Rustication. Mode of building masonry. Individual blocks of courses of stone have deeply recessed joints and often a roughened surface. *Banded:* horizontal joints emphasized. *Chamfered:* stones are smooth but have V-joints. *Rock-faced:* stones have irregular surface and appear unhewn. *Vermiculated:* stone given appearance of being worm-eaten.

Reconstruction. To rebuild according to original plans or drawings.

Rotunda. A round building or internal space, circular or oval in plan and usually domed. Greek Revival.

Shed Dormer. A dormer window with a horizontal eave line.

Stretcher. A brick or stone laid with its length parallel to the face of the wall.

Turret. Small decorative tower usually set on the ridge of a gable roof.

Tympanum. Triangular or segmental space between enclosing moldings of a pediment. Greek Revival.

Index

Page numbers in *italics* indicate illustrations